THE
NIGHTMARE
DICTIONARY

THE
NIGHTMARE
DICTIONARY

Falling elevators, lost teeth, slithering snakes, and everything else that keeps you up at night

Discover what causes nightmares and what your bad dreams mean

Aadamsmedia

Avon, Massachusetts

Published by
Adams Media, a division of F+W Media, Inc.
57 Littlefield Street, Avon, MA 02322. U.S.A.
www.adamsmedia.com

Contains material adapted and abridged from: *The Everything® Dreams Book, 2nd Edition* by Jenni Kosarin, copyright © 2005, 1998 by F+W Media, Inc., ISBN 10: 1-59337-336-8, ISBN 13: 978-1-59337-336-8; *The Everything® Lucid Dreaming Book* by Michael R. Hathaway, DCH, copyright © 2012 by F+W Media, Inc., ISBN 10: 1-4405-2855-1, ISBN 13: 978-1-4405-2855-2; *The Complete Dream Dictionary* by Trish and Rob MacGregor, copyright © 2004 by F+W Media, Inc., ISBN 10: 1-59337-109-8, ISBN 13: 978-1-59337-109-8; and *The Everything® Law of Attraction Dream Dictionary* by Cathleen O'Connor, copyright © 2010 by F+W Media, Inc., ISBN 10: 1-4405-0466-0, ISBN 13: 978-1-4405-0466-2.

ISBN 10: 1-4405-6017-X
ISBN 13: 978-1-4405-6017-0
eISBN 10: 1-4405-6018-8
eISBN 13: 978-1-4405-6018-7

Printed in the United States of America.

10   9   8   7   6   5   4   3   2   1

This book is available at quantity discounts for bulk purchases.
For information, please call 1-800-289-0963.

CONTENTS

INTRODUCTION

WHAT GOES BUMP
IN THE NIGHT

I t happens to everyone. Suddenly you're being chased by a terrifying monster through a dark alleyway. You're being buried alive, and fighting to breathe through dirt. You're falling from an incredibly tall building to the busy street below.

Then you're back in your bed, covered in a cold sweat. Even though you're safe, you can't quite shake the feeling that you're about to get eaten, suffocated, or flattened.

It was only a dream, you tell yourself. *Only a bad dream.*

You spend about a third of your life asleep. That means that in a lifespan of seventy-five years, you sleep the equivalent of twenty-five years. You dream for about 20 percent of your sleeping life. That's five years of dreams!

Some of those dreams can be wonderful—you see people you love, you achieve goals you've been striving for, you enter a wonderful fantasyland. But many dreams are dark, scary, and confusing. The possibility of five years of nightmares is daunting.

"It was only a dream" is what you say to children when they wake up from a nightmare. But is it right to dismiss them so casually? Nightmares can be very important. They've inspired great works of art and they've helped dreamers to predict terrible tragedies.

If good dreams reflect your hopes and desires, nightmares often reveal your deepest fears and anxieties. Sometimes you already know what your nightmares mean—if you have dreams about failing an important test you've been studying for, that dream reflects your fear that you have not prepared enough.

But many nightmares are not so clear. If you're being chased by a monster, what are you really afraid of? Or what if you have that dream about failing an important test, but you've been out of school for years? Sometimes, nightmares bring to light issues that you've pushed deep down into your subconscious.

This book will help you interpret your nightmares, no matter how bizarre they might be. You'll learn the hidden meanings of common bad dreams. Once you know why your nightmares are happening, you can use them to conquer your waking fears.

You'll also learn how to use lucid dreaming to take control of your nightmares. Once you've mastered this technique, you'll know that you're dreaming while in the midst of even the most horrifying nightmare. Even better, you'll be able to act independently and change your environment. With lucid dreaming you can resolve your anxieties while you're still in your dream—without even opening your eyes.

With these strategies, you'll stop dreading nightmares. Instead, you'll look forward to these dreams as powerful and important journeys of self-discovery. And instead of waking up in a cold sweat, you'll wake up with a new understanding of how your mind works.

PART 1
Exploring Nightmares

CHAPTER 1

YOUR NIGHTMARE AND YOU

The average person will have more than 100,000 dreams in his or her lifetime. At least some of those dreams are going to be nightmares. All too often, bad dreams can affect your waking hours, making you skittish or tired. If you are especially prone to nightmares, just the idea of going to sleep may begin to frighten you.

The first step in dealing with these frightening and confusing dreams is to understand them. In this chapter, you will first learn about the different categories of nightmares. You will also learn about the most common bad dreams and how to interpret them. You may be surprised to discover how universal your nightmares are, and how easily even the most bizarre visions can be pulled apart and broken down into understandable parts. Lastly, you will learn how to analyze your own nightmares, even the most unusual ones. And you'll find ancient practices of resolving your dreams, methods that have worked for centuries.

The Pet's Dream

Studies have shown that all humans dream, but so do all animals—even your pets! All birds and mammals dream. Strangely enough, cold-blooded animals are the only ones that don't dream.

Categorizing Your Nightmares

Not all bad dreams are created equally. How can you tell the difference between a nightmare that's a warning and a bad dream that's just cleaning out the cobwebs? You may experience different kinds of nightmares. In this section you will learn about these various types, how to identify them, and what might cause them.

Release Nightmares

Even though fear, insecurity, frustration, and angst often cannot be expressed during waking hours, some part of you always needs to be heard. Your regrets, worries, and concerns—things you find too difficult to deal with consciously—go straight to your subconscious and come through in release dreams. Release nightmares are typically jumbled. They have no sequential order and are often terrifying or nerve-racking for the dreamer. When you're being chased or running away from something evil, you are usually having a release dream. Experts say that the monster or demon you're running from is actually yourself. Do you want the release dream, the nightmare, to go away? Confront the part of your life that needs work, and these evil beings will leave you alone.

Remember to ask yourself important life questions before you go to sleep. When you recall your dreams the next morning, something in your nighttime visions should give you an answer to your dilemma.

Nightmares That Heal

Though many dream experts say it's important to remember your dreams, others say it's equally important to forget them. Francis Crick, a Nobel Prize winner who co-discovered the double helix, studied dreams with Graeme Mitchison. The two determined that dreams and nightmares are the brain's only way of wiping itself clean and preparing for new tasks ahead. In fact, they say, when you dream your mind erases and deletes certain obsessive, controlling tendencies.

Dreaming also enables incorrect information—ideas that you've changed in your conscious mind to accommodate an idealistic view of things—to right itself. It seems that the brain's neocortex, where memory is stored, must "unload."

Letting Go Through the Nightmare

If you're obsessing about something in waking life—such as a relationship that's on its way out—you're probably having nightmares about it. Don't try to overanalyze these dreams. Let it go! Your subconscious can work it out for you.

Recurring Nightmares

What causes a repetitious nightmare? There can be several different reasons. A nightmare may have its roots in a traumatic event that you experienced sometime during your life. If you have experienced such an event, it may replay itself in your mind, both when you are awake and when you dream.

It is possible you may have had an experience at a point in your life that you do not consciously remember, and it continues to haunt you in your nightmares. Your unconscious mind takes everything in and does remember, playing it out again in your dreams. More than one event in your life may trigger your nightmares, so it is feasible that lucid dreaming may help you trace your nightmares back to an earlier incident.

Some dream experts say that if you're having the same nightmare over and over again, it could be that your soul recognizes something you've already been through and is still trying to work it out. In other words, this is where reincarnation truly could show itself. A recurring dream, experts say, can simply be made of past-life memories. You may have suffered a traumatic event in another life that resurfaces in your current life in the form of a nightmare.

Dreaming of your own death is almost never prophetic. As you'll learn later, usually a dream about death signifies change, transition, or upheaval. Occasionally, however, souls do remember *previous* deaths, and they replay them in nightmares over and over again until the subconscious accepts it. It's almost like getting stuck in a time warp. Your mind, without your consciousness to filter in who you are now, remembers who it once was.

Phobias from Another Life

Fears and phobias can be connected to a past-life traumatic situation. When such feelings come on suddenly, they create an altered state of consciousness, similar to a nightmare, except that the person experiencing the trauma is actually hallucinating. You could consider this experience a waking nightmare.

Don't try to analyze these dreams with questions like, "Why do they keep chasing me?" or "Why do I keep waking up when I'm about to die?" Let your subconscious work out the memory, and eventually it will simply go away.

Sometimes it helps to tell a close friend or relative about a recurring nightmare. By acknowledging it, you admit that it's happening. This can help get the burden off your shoulders so you can move on with your waking life.

Different Nightmares with the Same Theme

It is also possible to experience nightmares that are different every time but still have a connection through a similar theme. For instance, you might always be running away from something. In one dream it might be an animal such as a tiger, lion, or bear that is trying to get you. In another it might be a bad guy doing the chasing. The result is that you usually wake up with your heart pounding.

These dreams may be caused by stress in your life or even by certain types of medication. Sometimes, your system is trying to make adjustments to medicine that you may have started taking or stopped taking. Other health conditions can cause nightmares as well. Your body may be sending you a message through your nightmares to pay attention to yourself.

Night Terrors

You've just turned out the light and are settling in for a good night's sleep when a bloodcurdling scream shreds the silence. You leap up and rush into your son's room and find him in a panic, completely disoriented. When you calm him down and question him, he tells you about a single, horrifying image of being crushed or strangled or attacked. And then, five minutes later, he's forgotten about the dream completely. The only thing that's left is his fear.

It isn't a nightmare that woke him, but a night terror. These debilitating dreams are even more intense and more powerful than nightmares. Anyone who's had one will not confuse it with a nightmare. Actually, these are most common in children between the ages of three and eight. Most children either remember nothing about what frightened them or recall only fragmented images, which is characteristic of what happens when you're awakened from the deepest stages of sleep. People who have suffered from post-traumatic stress syndrome, from war or a violent attack, have probably also experienced night terrors.

What Are the Symptoms of Night Terrors?

The person who has had a night terror is almost impossible to calm down and the next day usually doesn't remember the dream images. He may also suffer from a fear of going to sleep, feelings of shame and horror about having night terrors, excessive heart rate, hot sweats, and confusion.

Ernest Hartmann, psychoanalyst and author of *The Nightmare*, says that night terrors sometimes run in families, suggesting the possibility of a genetic susceptibility.

They usually last about five to twenty minutes, and they happen in one of the deepest levels of sleep. It's not known why some people don't grow out of night terrors, but, Hartmann adds, "Some adults with night terrors have been noted to have phobic or obsessive personalities." Therefore, it's also possible that night terrors run in families with similar beliefs and thought processes.

Most people who have night terrors are unable or unwilling to notice or express strong feelings in the daytime. This is why people with post-traumatic stress disorder or intense stress have them more frequently. "The night terror episodes may express a kind of outbreak of repressed emotion," Hartmann says.

Prophetic (Psychic) Message Nightmares

In 1865, Abraham Lincoln dreamed that he heard strange sounds coming from the East Room of the White House. When he investigated, he saw a corpse resting on a catafalque, a funeral platform. He saw soldiers standing around the body, guarding it, while a throng of people looked on. The face was covered, so Lincoln asked one of the guards who had died. "The president," the guard replied. A week later, Lincoln was assassinated.

Another prophecy was reported in the May 13, 1956, issue of *Parade* magazine: "As for the 1960 election, Mrs. (Jeane) Dixon thinks it will be dominated by labor and won by a Democrat. But he will be assassinated or die in office, though not necessarily in his first term." Jeane Dixon was, of course, talking about John Kennedy. Even though Dixon was wrong about other things, this prediction tended to stick in people's minds. She won acclaim and credibility from it.

While speaking at the Miami Book Fair one year, author Anne Rice told the heartbreaking story of how she had come to write *Interview with the Vampire*.

She dreamed that her young daughter was dying of a blood disease. Shortly afterward, the girl was diagnosed with leukemia. In the aftermath of her daughter's death, Rice wrote *Interview with the Vampire* in a feverish frenzy in just three weeks, as though it were a kind of purging. It's probably no coincidence that blood is the theme of the book.

In the next dream, a hillside is the setting for a glimpse of a young man's death. This dream is called "The Hillside":

> *John and I are sitting on a grassy hillside overlooking a valley. I'm not real sure what we're doing here or how we came to be here, but that doesn't seem to matter in the dream. We're talking about people we knew in college and the crazy things we did. Suddenly he turns to me and says, "It's time for me to move on. But don't worry about me. I'll be in touch."*
>
> *The next morning, I remembered dreaming about him and figured the dream meant he would be showing up any day now. He was nomadic in that sense,*

taking off when he felt like it, hitching around the country and dropping in on friends, who were always glad to see him. I kept thinking that I should call our mutual friend, Linda, who usually knew where he was. But that evening, Linda called me in tears. John had been killed in a car accident the night before.

Several years later, the woman dreamed that she and John met on the same hillside, talking and laughing again about old times. Then he suddenly turned to her and said he was "moving on to the next level." She hasn't dreamed of him in the more than twenty years since. Apparently, he really was "moving on." There is nothing to analyze in this dream. It should be taken as a real message from John.

In the case of John and the hillside dream, there was nothing the dreamer could do to prevent the death. But some near-death dreams can serve as warnings. You dream, for example, that the plane you're supposed to take tomorrow crashes and because of the dream, you change your flight. Then you hear that something really did happen. Though they are possible, these dreams are extremely rare.

Frightening prophetic dreams unfold logically, with events that happen in sequential order. Many psychics also say that prophecy dreams only happen in color and that they're incredibly vivid as well. Here's an interesting tidbit: You don't have to be psychic at all in order to have a prophecy dream. If fact, many people who are psychic or incredibly intuitive in their waking hours may never have a prophecy dream, whereas those who have prophecy dreams are not necessarily psychic in waking life.

Knowing the Future

It's impossible to know the future instantly, without work. Dreams are good indications of what can happen, but they don't always reveal what will happen. It's up to you to interpret them and then shape your future. That's the surest way of obtaining results. With practice, signs and guideposts will become easier to recognize.

Psychic dreams are often intense and, because of their nature, can cause anxiety for the dreamer. When children or teenagers have tragic psychic dreams, they often feel somehow responsible for events that actually happen. Consequently, they try to suppress their psychic abilities and often live and sleep in fear that they will have another dream about tragedy.

Prophecy nightmares can be confusing because they usually deliver a warning, but the dreamer is not always given enough information to take action. Be patient if this happens to you. Ask out loud for more assistance just before you go to sleep the next night, and the next, until you get it. Never dismiss your bad dreams. If you get a warning that something may happen to your brother in his car, for example, make sure you tell him to be careful driving. Even if he thinks you're nuts, you'll still feel better later.

Inspirational Nightmares

Stephen King's book *Misery* was based on a bad dream he had. Frankenstein's Monster came alive in a nightmare Mary Shelley had after discussing reanimation with her future husband.

Nightmares can be scary, yes, but they can also be fantastical and creative. Don't be afraid to use the images that frighten you as daytime inspirations.

Remembering Your Nightmares

Many people don't want to remember their nightmares. But if your subconscious is trying to tell you something, it might be a good idea to learn how to listen. The best way to remember dreams is to record them right after they end. If you don't usually wake up after a dream, try giving yourself a suggestion before you go to sleep to awaken after a dream. It is possible using this technique to recall four or five dreams a night. Remembering dreams just takes practice.

Examining Your Nightmares

Nightmares can be so strange and unfathomable. How do you begin to interpret them? Many times you'll get a number, but you won't know if it's a date, a measure of time, or even an amount of money. Here are some techniques you can use to translate the symbols in your dreams.

Metaphors

Metaphors are figures of speech that substitute one image with another to suggest a connection between the two; "buried in work" is a metaphor. When you recognize a metaphor in your dreams, it can help a perplexing image take on meaning. For example, when you dream about people in your life, think about what they represent to you. If Bert from your office is a gossip, his appearance in a dream might refer to gossip.

Here's another example. A woman who had been reading tarot cards before going to bed dreamed that she was at a turnstile in a subway station. The token she put in didn't go through. A hand reached into her vision and held out a vividly colored tarot card—Strength—which she then inserted into the slot. The turnstile began to move and she was able to pass through with ease. The turnstile, she felt, was a metaphor for how she was about to undergo a "turn" or change in her "style" of doing certain things; hence, "turnstile." The Strength card practically proclaimed that she possessed the inner resources to make the change success-fully. Deep down, she knew she could handle it.

Edgar Cayce said, "All dreams are given for the benefit of the individual, would he but interpret them correctly." Some significant dream metaphors for your life might be "in the dark" (a secret or the truth is hidden from you) or "turbulent waters" (usually indicating a relationship on the brink of disaster).

Puns

Another way to decipher meaning is to think of a dream as a pun, or a play on words. For example, a dream of Bob Hope bouncing along on a pogo stick, moving off into the distance, might seem outrageous and nonsensical. However, a look at the dream elements as a sort of pun reveals a message: Hope springs eternal. If a bizarre image or random person ever appears in your dreams, thinking of the situation as a pun could help expose its true meaning.

Archetypes

An archetype is a symbol or theme that rises from a layer of the mind common to all people. Carl Jung called this layer the collective unconscious, and he believed that each of us gives these symbols and themes our own individual stamp. Archetypes are prevalent in mythology, folklore, and religion. The hero, for instance, is a common theme in mythology that has been transferred to forms of modern media, such as movies. Archetypes always relate to a higher meaning.

Always look for the big picture before you start going into details. Then, when you're finished pinpointing the general meaning of an archetype, relate it to how you feel about that meaning. Does it make sense for you?

Interpreting Common Nightmares

When you read through the nightmare dictionary found later in this book, you'll recognize many of the words as common fixtures in your own nightmares. Research suggests that increased levels of anxiety in waking life can increase the frequency and intensity of nightmares. What nightmares really do is invade your dream state to work out problems unresolved in waking life. Some common nightmare symbols include guns, thieves, ghosts, demons, monsters, and the devil. These symbols translate into different meanings for each person. The importance lies in the context of the dream.

Snakes

Read the following nightmare and think about how you would react. Before reading the translation of the dream that follows, try to decipher what it could mean and why the dreamer may have dreamed it. This dream is called "Snakes":

I'm walking in tall grass, grass that brushes my knees. I hear rustling around me and pick up my pace, anxious to get to the clearing I can see just ahead. I know the rustling is caused by snakes.

The rustling gets louder, like the cacophony of a thousand crickets screaming for rain. I start running. I'm still running when I reach the clearing and run right into a bed of snakes. They are everywhere, writhing, slithering, rattling. But even worse than the snakes is the realization that I'm barefoot and that the only way I'm going to get out of this is to walk through them. So I walk. And I make it through the bed of snakes without getting bitten.

In the ancient Greek and Roman cultures, snakes were symbols of the healing arts. In the Bible, the snake symbolizes temptation and forbidden knowledge. In fairy tales, the snake is often a trickster—wise but wily. The ancient symbol of the snake swallowing its own tail represents the way nature feeds on and renews itself. Jung considered snakes to be archetypal, representing an awareness of the essential energy of life and nature.

The woman who had this dream was in the process of breaking away from a Catholic background. She wanted to explore areas her religion would call heretical. Therefore, she needed to apply her beliefs and feelings at the time she had the dream to this particular archetype. What could it mean?

She interpreted the dream to mean that the prospect of this exploration was somewhat frightening for her, but that she would complete it without harm. She felt the dream was confirming her belief that the exploration was a necessary step in her growth as a human being.

On another level, though, she felt the dream was pointing to a situation at work, one in which she was surrounded by "snakes in the grass"—a pun that probably indicated malicious gossip. Because the snakes didn't bite her, she figured she would not be hurt by whatever was being said about her.

Even though the snake is considered an archetypal symbol, in this case the most relevant meaning to the dreamer concerned her daily life. She didn't need a psychologist to interpret the dream for her. Once she'd remembered it and written it down, the pun "clicked" for her. She knew what the dream was referring to. Pay attention to your gut when translating your dreams. You'll find the solution. Guaranteed.

Death Dreams

You wake up in a sweat. In your dream, you were running from a mugger or robbers or even the devil himself. And you were just about to die. *Thank goodness I woke up!* you think. You wipe your brow and remember that old wives' tale that if you die in your dream, you also die in real life. What blarney! Don't believe it. Dreaming of death rarely means you or someone you dreamed about is going to die. Sometimes people actually do die in their dreams, dream of their own funerals, or even view themselves dead from above. But the vast majority of these dreamers have lived to tell about it.

The Devil in the Details

Dreaming about the devil doesn't necessarily signify evil. Many times, the devil means marriage. If you're married, the devil usually represents your other half. Examine how you feel toward the devil in the dream, and you'll understand how you feel about your partner.

True, in very rare situations, a person could dream of his own death and know it was going to happen. But one thing must be understood. In dreams, time and space don't exist. A person can have visits from a departed loved one, for example, who's trying to get her accustomed to the idea of dying. But the person on the other side has no concept of time—death might be five, ten, twenty, or thirty years away. Most likely, if it's a prophetic dream—in sequential order and in vivid color—it's not referring to anything that can happen soon.

Only rarely do death dreams portend an actual physical death. In the following dream, which deals with the living and the dead, the dream is more about the woman's future life than her death. Laura, a forty-five-year-old woman, had asked for a dream to confirm that things in her life were "clicking along" as they should be. Laura had the following dream, called "Community Theater":

> I'm in a barn-like structure, perhaps a community theater. Both the living and the dead are here, as though this is some sort of meeting place between worlds or dimensions. A woman informs me that by punching in my birth date information, I can find out anything about myself or my life that I need to know.
>
> There are people here who travel about in both the world of the living and the world of the dead. One such woman tells me that one day, the "glass" between the borders of life and death will be so clear that I'll be able to "see" through it.
>
> The dream ends with a fire drill. My former head-mistress sticks her head in and orders everyone to get outside.

The dreamer was an amateur astrologer, so the birth date reference made sense to her. She interpreted it as a message to do a progressed astrological chart for herself for the coming year. She also felt this was a clear message from her unconscious that everything she needed to know was available to her in the dream state; all she had to do was ask. It reassured her that her unconscious was always accessible and that she already possessed tools in her waking life to clarify issues and questions.

When Laura related the dream to her husband, he told her that the birth date reference sounded like a computerized akashic record, the "cosmic" record that seer Edgar Cayce said he accessed during his readings. The dreamer felt that the "glass" that separated the living and the dead was the dream state. The fire drill at the end of the dream was literally a wakeup call, prodding her to consciousness so that she would record the dream.

Death in your nightmares often represents change. Death is the ultimate metamorphosis, the passage from one state of being to another. In the tarot, for example, the Death card doesn't mean death. It means transformation—a major change that hurls you from one way of life to another. In a dream, death usually means the same thing. "Ninety-nine percent of the time, dreams about death are simply metaphors for major changes happening in your relationships, work, or personality," writes Stase Michaels in *The Bedside Guide to Dreams*.

When you have a death dream, ask yourself whether an area of your life is undergoing transformation. Are you in the middle of a divorce? About to have a baby? About to get married? Are you considering a career change? Any of these big life decisions can prompt a death dream.

Moving on to the Other Side

If you have a dream about a departed loved one who says she's okay or moving on, chances are that this person really did come to visit you and means just that—she's happy.

Often, dreams about death involve other symbols. A car, for instance, is a perfect dream metaphor for where you're going in life and how the journey is unfolding. For a sixteen-year-old girl, a death dream involving a car was a result of her family's recent move from the state where she'd been born and raised. For a forty-eight-year-old accountant, a dream about death was caused by a major job transition from a large firm to self-employment.

In the next dream, the death symbolism pointed to a young man's changing feelings about his girlfriend. The name of this dream is "Carnival":

> *Jan and I are at the carnival that's rolled into town. It was her idea to go and she's like a kid, eating cotton candy, running from ride to ride, insistent that I go with her. I don't like carnivals and wish we could leave. She wants to go on the roller coaster; I don't.*

*We argue out there in front of everyone and I'm
totally embarrassed. Just to keep her quiet, I relent
and go on the roller coaster with her.*

*I hate the roller coaster, everyone screaming, Jan
clutching my arm and shrieking like a five-year-old.
As our car speeds down one of the hills in the track,
Jan's seat restraint suddenly snaps open and she's
hurled out of the car. I see her shooting like a missile
through the air and know it's going to kill her. I feel
relieved.*

*When I woke up, I was shocked at my lack of emo-
tion and couldn't go back to sleep. But the longer I lay
there, the clearer it became that she and I no longer
enjoyed the same things, that she was immature, and
that for me the relationship was already over. Ending
it was merely a formality.*

The Family Nightmare

Dream dictionaries argue that to dream of members of
your extended family is not always positive. To dream of a
cousin, the experts sometimes say, indicates you might have
disappointment and sadness. Even dreaming of a friendly
correspondence with your cousin signifies that there might
be a major falling out in the family. If a woman dreams of
her aunt, supposedly, she will soon receive severe criticism
about the choices and actions she makes in life. However,

dreams of death and sex involving family members may have very different connotations.

A death or near-death dream involving a family member or relative, like most death dreams, may point to a major upheaval in the dreamer's life. The dream acts as a conduit of information, as in the next example. This dream is called "Apparition":

> *Aunt Pat, my mother's older sister, appears to me, hovering like a ghost in a corner of the bedroom. In the dream, the image is so clear I can see the lines in her face, the soft gray of her hair, the shape of her mouth. She's speaking to me, but I can't hear the words.*
>
> *I suddenly associate this kind of apparition with stories I've heard about departed people who appear to loved ones at the time of their deaths. I try to scream, but can't, and bolt awake. For seconds it seems that the image of my aunt is actually in a corner of the bedroom, exactly where it was in the dream. Then I blink and the apparition fades. Or maybe it wasn't really there at all; maybe I imagined it. I still don't know.*
>
> *The next day, I called my parents and asked if my aunt was okay. As far as they knew she was. I forgot about the dream until several days later, when my parents said they'd spoken to my aunt. She had fallen*

*and cracked her hip over the same weekend I had the
dream and was planning on moving in with her son.*

Despite immediate evidence to the contrary, this dream
indicated that the aunt would be or was already undergoing a major life change. Though in the dream she's a sort
of ghost—which the dreamer then translated as her aunt
being dead and coming to visit her—this isn't the case.
Instead, the aunt was about to move in with her son. She
was making a drastic life change. This is an example of a
precognitive death dream. The dreamer dreamed about the
aunt dying or appearing as a ghost; instead, the aunt was
actually about to go through a life transition.

Falling Nightmares

Dreams of falling may be metaphors for the fallen
woman or man, a fall from grace, or the fall season. The
interpretation depends, to a large extent, on what is going
on in your life. It can even refer to what happened to you
within the twenty-four hours preceding the dream.

One young married woman dreamed she was falling
from a building. It later struck her as a metaphor for her
affair with a married man from her office. The fall, she said,
didn't just represent a fall from grace; it was what would
happen to her marriage if her husband discovered the affair.

Quite often such a dream will have that "zing" to it, and
you'll immediately know the reference. But other times, its

meaning may be as obscure as the solution to a complex mathematical equation. You'll have to take it apart piece by piece, and then you must figure out how to put it all together.

Derek, an actor, dreamed he was in a convertible with his agent, who was driving. While they were speeding along a country road, the car hit a deep hole and veered out of control. His agent, a woman, slammed her foot on the brake, but the brakes failed and they plunged over the side of a cliff.

This dream could have been interpreted many ways. But the only one that mattered was the one that made sense to Derek—the one that offered him new insight into his relationship with his agent. He mulled the dream over for a day or two and realized that for quite a while he'd felt as if she had mishandled his career and he wasn't able to "apply the brake" to the downward spiral in his relationship with her. He ended their partnership several days later—a split that was, for him, like a plunge over the edge of a cliff into an abyss of the unknown.

What Are You Feeling?

Dream therapist Gayle Delaney suggests that you ask yourself how you feel in your dream as you're falling. Do you feel terrified? Helpless? Out of control? Or is the sensation pleasant? If so, how? These responses can be clues to what the falling means for you.

As a sort of exercise, jot down a recurring falling dream you've had. If it was recent, note what was going on in your life at the time of the dream. Had you just reached a crossroads in a relationship? Was an important partnership in the throes of change? Had your children recently left home? Did you, previously, have a drug or an alcohol habit? Interpret the dream. Note if a decision was made as a result of this dream. Let the dream speak to you. Write down:

- The date and time you had the dream
- The action of the dream
- The events immediately preceding the dream
- Your interpretation

Test-Taking and Classroom Nightmares

Jim, a self-employed contractor, dreamed that he was hurrying to make an 8:00 A.M. class. When he got there, the professor was passing out final exam booklets. He realized that he'd been to the class only a couple times the entire semester and that he wasn't prepared for the exam.

Although it had been more than twenty years since Jim graduated from college, he had this dream once or twice a year. The specifics rarely changed. Once he began to record and study his dreams, however, he understood that the dream usually occurred when he was facing a bid on a major project. Even though he spent weeks preparing figures on a prospective project, he rarely felt adequately prepared.

How Old Are You in the Dream?

It's interesting to note what age you are in the dream. Are you the age you were when you were in school or the age you are now? If you're the age you are now, the test-taking dream is a metaphor for something you're currently experiencing.

For most of us, the examination dream follows a format similar to Jim's. In *The Dream Game*, Ann Faraday notes that most of these dreams occur when we feel we're being tested or examined by someone, as in a job interview, for example. Everyone feels unprepared at one time or another. The examination dream is often a reflection of an uneasy sensation of not being ready for something coming into your life.

When interpreting this type of dream, make note of whether you have an important deadline or are under extreme pressure in your waking life. If you're not, then ask yourself whether you feel unprepared to cope with something in your life. In your dream journal, don't forget to record the dream in detail.

When you dream of being in a classroom, examine your surroundings and your reason for being there. Do you have a positive feeling about the learning environment? Do you recognize the person teaching the class? What is the subject matter you're learning? Often, a classroom dream relates to a personal growth period you're going through.

A thirty-three-year-old woman who had recently joined a dream group related the following classroom dream. The dream had occurred eleven years earlier, when she was in college, and it had always puzzled her. She asked if anyone in the dream group had any idea what it could mean. As you read through this dream, take special note of the way the woman describes the lobby and classroom. This dream is titled "The Next Step":

> *My friend Tanya and I are sitting in a lobby with perhaps a dozen other people of various ages and races. We aren't sure why we're there. There's nothing about the lobby to tell me exactly where it is. I feel very uneasy about this place. I go up to the information desk and ask the receptionist what we're waiting for.*
>
> *"For the class to begin," she replies.*
>
> *"I didn't sign up for a class," I tell her.*
>
> *"You must have. You're here."*
>
> *Then she goes back to whatever she was doing, and I return to my seat. Not long afterward, she calls my name and Tanya's. We file into a college-style auditorium. It's crowded with people and brightly lit by a*

skylight. The color of the sky is odd, a kind of glowing cerulean blue.

The speaker is a well-known literary figure, whose name I forgot when I woke up but whom I knew had died some years before. I suddenly realize I am in an afterlife classroom, about to be oriented to dying and to whatever happens next.

Several members of the dream group immediately associated the dream with reports from near-death survivors. The dreamer herself agreed, but she pointed out that no one had died around the time she'd had the dream and that she had never had a near-death experience. In fact, at the time of the dream, Raymond Moody's seminal book on near-death experiences, *Life After Life*, hadn't yet been published.

But the dream confirmed her belief in the survival of consciousness and triggered a lifelong interest in metaphysical topics. The dream recurs periodically, usually when the woman experiences a crisis of faith in her spiritual beliefs. But it always renews her belief in the path she has chosen.

When a teacher has a classroom dream, on the other hand, the meaning might be more practical than symbolic. This was the case in the following dream related by Bharata, the sixty-six-year-old director of the Yoga & Inner Peace studio in Lake Worth, Florida. He dreamed he was the only teacher for two classes that were scheduled to meet at the same time, and he had to teach both classes, running back and forth from room to room.

In Bharata's case, the classroom dream was a reflection of his inner concern that he was teaching too many classes. Although he enjoyed teaching, his schedule included two or three classes a day, and he had been considering adding other teachers to lighten his load.

The Afterlife

Afterlife dreams can be tricky because nine times out of ten, they're really visits to the Other Side—trips our subconscious refuses to acknowledge as real. These dreams are gifts. Write them down.

Nudity Nightmares

In *The Dream Game*, Ann Faraday writes of a young man's dream of being naked in front of a cheering crowd. In the dream, he was exhilarated. What were the circumstances going on in his waking life? Well, he had recently had his first experience of sexual intercourse, and for him the dream meant that he had shed his moral prohibitions. "Had the onlookers in the dream been disapproving, this would have indicated guilt feelings; for in the objective world, his fellow students would certainly have approved," Faraday wrote.

Dreams in which you're naked indicate a need to express yourself. Fears, inhibitions, and classic "exposing yourself" issues come up in an instant. The key is to examine how you feel in the dream about your nudity. Do you feel good? Free? Scared? Nude dreams don't always refer to actually being naked. Sometimes you have problems in which you feel vulnerable, and your fears translate into and liberate themselves as nude dreams.

If you have a nude dream in which you feel silly or scared, ask yourself these questions in your waking life:

- Is there an issue right now you're not facing?
- How do you feel weak?
- To whom do you feel susceptible?
- How can you rectify this problem?

Work toward facing the person and the problem directly, and you'll find that the issue fades away. You'll feel better and more in control of your life. Don't let others treat you without the respect you deserve. Nude dreams in which you feel exposed are often the result of feeling inadequate or insecure about your position in life.

Nightmares about a Lost Purse, Wallet, Keys, or Briefcase

Purses and wallets usually contain credit cards, money, and identification—these are important. In fact, they're society's evidence of who you are. Keys open doors, start your car, and allow you entrance to your home and office. Briefcases typically contain papers related to work. In some ways, these things define you. They're your personal possessions—yours alone. Therefore, says Gayle Delaney, this dream can occur among women whose children have recently left home. Typically, these dreams also occur among men who have retired or who have been fired from their jobs.

Dreams of lost personal items are frequently reported by people in transition from one way of life or mode of thought to another. This has to do with a shift in perceived identity. Pay close attention to these dreams.

Losing personal objects in dreams can also indicate a lack of dedication to your responsibilities. When you don't feel like you have control over the things that are important, it gets translated in your dreams as the loss of personal possessions.

Bills Bills Bills!

If you're having dreams about losing your wallet, you'd better check your bills! Your subconscious knows that something needs to be paid and is anxious about it.

Another factor may be that in your waking life, you feel like you're not taking care of your financial obligations. The loss of a purse or a wallet in dreams sometimes indicates how you feel about your monetary situation. Closely examine what you're taking care of and what you're not. Most likely, you'll come up with the solution quickly.

Traveling Nightmares

Having a bad dream about traveling could relate to stress concerning an upcoming trip. But if you have no plans for a journey, your dream sojourn may be a symbolic one. Pay particular attention to details about your trip. Where are you going? Are you traveling alone or with others? Do you have luggage with you? Keep in mind that what happens on your trip might be more important than the destination.

A newspaper reporter named Jerry related the following recurring dream. This dream is called "Missing Connections":

> I'm taking a train in a foreign country and must transfer from one train to another. The problem is that I've lost track of my luggage. I'm looking all over for it, and I know I must hurry or I'll miss the connecting train. Sometimes I'm in a train station without my luggage, which is still on the train I just got off. I usually wake up before I find out what happens.

After discussing the dream with friends, Jerry saw two possible meanings for the dream. In both of them, the journey was his job. Although he didn't travel much, his work relied on making connections with sources for stories. His fear was that he wouldn't make contact with his sources or that, when he reached them, he wouldn't be ready for the interview. His luggage represented his preparation for the interview.

The other interpretation involved the question of his future as a reporter. Jerry was tired of chasing down stories day after day and wanted to make a career change. But he feared that he was not prepared to make the change and that he would miss his connection to a new career.

The Missed Connection Nightmare

If you have an anxiety dream in which you keep missing your travel connection to meet up with a boyfriend, a girlfriend, or a lover, it indicates anxiety about the relationship. Ask yourself why this might be, and examine the situation.

Nightmares about Losing Teeth

A dream about losing teeth is telling you something about yourself. It could reflect a feeling of being out of control—like your life has no order to it. Because losing teeth or hair is such a natural thing, something that can happen to anyone, your subconscious makes it a very real possibility in your dreams. But it's metaphoric.

Ann Faraday notes that her own tooth-loss dreams "almost always reflect my feeling that I have 'lost face' or 'spoiled my self-image' in some way during the day; usually by giving in to emotions of fear or weakness." Edgar Cayce viewed dreams of losing teeth as metaphors for loose or careless speech. In this case, you might regret gossiping about someone. Women are said to have this sort of dream more than men.

Why Do I Keep Having the "Teeth Falling Out" Dream?

If you keep having this dream, it means you're stuck in a particular pattern because some unresolved issue in your life has gotten out of control. Ask yourself what that may be. Have you been gossiping about someone? Are you not sure which way to go with your career? Do your homework and you'll find the answer.

If the suggested interpretations of the previous dream don't work for you, ask yourself what teeth mean to you. Do they represent power? A nice appearance? Aggressiveness? What is it that makes you feel toothless? Do teeth symbolize something to you? It's important to ask yourself these questions.

If you're having this or some of the other popular dreams, involving nudity, traveling, losing personal possessions, or taking a test, don't worry. We all have them. What's interesting is that common dream themes, like society itself, undoubtedly change over time. For the children of today, new topics may include UFOs and/or alien abductions, computer system crashes, extreme weather, airplane disasters, or other popular media topics. Still, the same message holds true. These common anxiety dreams will continue until you take control of their sources. Do it today.

Analyzing and Resolving Your Nightmares

Ask any three-year-old about her nightmares, and she'll probably tell you about dreams in which she's being pursued by terrifying animals—fire-breathing dragons, ferocious wolves, or dangerous lions.

Quite often, children's nightmares can happen after a scolding or punishment by parents. They also occur when a child is ill or in a transitional phase—during her parents' divorce or a move from one home to another, for example. Sometimes they seem to happen for no apparent external reason, though usually there's something at the core of it. If you gently interview children about their nightmares, you can usually get to the source.

But as children grow older, their nightmares change. Instead of threats and pursuits by animals, the scary encounter might be with a bully in school or a neighbor down the street. These nightmares often deal with real anxieties and fears children have in their waking lives.

In *The Bedside Guide to Dreams*, Stase Michaels outlines different kinds of nightmares that are common to adults. "In the first kind, you face your actual fears. In the second, you deal with pain and trauma in yourself and in your life. The third kind is the most common type of dream and is reflected in the saying 'I have met the enemy, and it is I.'"

In this last type of nightmare, you encounter a part of yourself you would rather not see. The person or event you're reacting to in your dream strikes an all-too-familiar chord because it reflects some element of yourself that you would rather keep hidden.

Sometimes, these nightmares seem to be literal warnings about something—your health, a personal relationship, or your career. But before you jump to any conclusions about your nightmare being a literal warning, exhaust the other possibilities.

Look for metaphors. Scrutinize the dream for hints that it illuminates some part of your personality you don't want to know about. Be honest. Does it depict one of your actual fears? Does it address a rejected part of you? Consider the following clues:

- **Vividness:** Warning dreams are usually very vivid.
- **Your reaction:** If a dream is a warning, you'll most likely react the same way you would react in waking life.
- **Similar details:** In a warning dream, your house looks like the actual house you live in. Your mother looks like your real mother. The dream has a literal feel that is lacking in the other kinds of dreams.

Confronting Fear

If you are often plagued by nightmares, the most important thing to do is confront your fears. Most people don't obsess about the things or situations they fear. They simply react when faced with the fear. Confronting your fears and emotions will help you to seize control of frightening situations in your dreams. It will also help you to work out your anxieties, which are most likely the root cause of the nightmares. By consciously recognizing what you fear, you take the first step in overcoming it.

In the nightmare that follows, the dreamer was living on the first floor of a condominium complex. Although the complex was safe, the neighborhood outside of it was one of the worst in town. Many people in the complex had security systems in their condos and in their cars. The dreamer didn't. The only thing that stood between her and the outside world were dead bolts on her doors. This dream is called "Dead Bolt":

> *I'm in the kitchen in the middle of the night, getting something to eat. Only the light over the stove is on. The door, which opens onto the condo courtyard, begins to rattle and I whip around. A horrible paralysis seizes me. I can't move or scream. I can only watch.*
>
> *A hand reaches inside the door. A man's hand. I can see the dirt under his fingernails. He is trying to reach the chain. I grab the teakettle and slam it against his fingers. His hand vanishes.*
>
> *I am looking at a broken dead bolt. I kick the door shut and fix a chair in front of it. I awaken in my bedroom, certain the man is out there in the courtyard now, and that he's going to try to break into the condo—my condo.*

This dream is literal, with no hidden meaning. The dreamer is being warned about the broken dead bolt on her kitchen door. She admitted that, for some time, the dead bolt had been broken and the entire locking mechanism could easily have been slipped out of the door, providing a peephole to the outside world. Right after she had the dream, she hired a locksmith to fix the door.

This dream possessed a vividness the dreamer recognized. It was also quite realistic. Her kitchen was depicted as it actually was. The dead bolt on the kitchen door was definitely broken, and the intruder's hand was rendered in astonishing detail. Two weeks later, a condo three doors down from hers was broken into.

Exercise for Nightmare Analysis

Categorize three nightmares you've had under broad topic headings like the ones presented in this chapter. Then define what these mean to you in your waking life. Do the definitions fit the dreams?

If these are recent dreams and you've recorded them in your journal, read them over. Note what was going on in your life at the time. Then interpret the dreams. Record the following:

- Broad categories and meanings
- Events in your life at the time of these dreams
- Your interpretations of the dreams

Sometimes, when we don't want to deal with these things head-on, they come full force into our dreams.

Exercise for Confronting Your Fear

Analyze one of your recurring nightmares. What are the prevalent images? Where does the dream take place? Are there any obvious metaphors or puns that may hold a vital clue to the meaning of the dream? How does the dream end? If you've never confronted your fear in this nightmare, rewrite the ending of the dream so that you do. Record:

- The nightmare
- The setting
- The metaphors
- How you act and react in the dream
- How you would change the dream

Your Waking Fears

Lynn, a thirty-year-old mother and photographer, was absolutely petrified of snakes until she got a photography assignment that took her to the Miami Serpentarium. The following is Lynn's description of how she conquered her fear:

> *Maybe it was seeing them through the lens of the camera. Maybe it was just that I was ready to deal with the fear. But, suddenly, I recognized their beauty, their incredible diversity. Toward the end of the assignment, one of the snake handlers brought over a boa he had worked with since it was born. I actually mustered the courage to touch it. And from that point on, I was no longer afraid of snakes.*

It often helps to recognize and admit your waking fears so you can overcome them in your sleep. Your dreams and nightmares can only do so much. If you have a very real fear of birds, for instance, images of birds or other animals will probably figure in your dreams and nightmares. You may have nightmares of big shadows hovering over you— or even ghosts—and not quite know what this means. But nightmares almost always translate back to very real fears you have in your waking life.

You can start breaking down your fears by performing a simple dream exercise. First, list five of your fears. Have any of these fears shown up in your dreams? Were they disguised as metaphorical images? Make a note of how you dealt with these fears in your dreams. Then outline a plan for conquering these fears in your waking life.

One woman had the following dream, called "Vampires":

> Last night I had a dream about girls I knew when I was about thirteen years old. I haven't seen or heard from them since. But even back then, we got along even though I never really was accepted into their clique. They were the "cool" girls, and I wanted to fit in.
>
> In the dream, I noticed that they were all vampires. We were all sitting around and I started feeling very uneasy. Then I eventually saw their fangs and one attacked me and started biting me and drawing blood. After that, I woke up.

Losing Blood

Losing blood in a dream usually refers to a loss of emotion or energy. If you bleed in a dream, you probably feel, in waking life, like you're being emotionally drained in some way. The presence of blood in a dream can also refer to life and matters of the heart.

After further investigation into this woman's feelings about her old friends, it was evident that there was really no hidden meaning here. These friends had been sucking energy from her back then (and she was wasting precious time with them)—hence, the blood-sucking reference. She remembered feeling left out, even though it had happened long ago.

What's important to analyze is not why these friends are coming back into her dreams, or even that she's having nightmares about them as vampires. Instead, she needs to ask herself other questions: Why now? What has reminded me of those isolated feelings? Who am I spending time with who isn't making me feel good about myself? Feelings of rejection constantly come up in nightmares. The important thing is to figure out why and to remove yourself from those people who can do serious harm to you emotionally.

Taking Control

The Senoi, a tribe that lives in the mountains of Malaysia, solved all their problems with dreams. Some say they had no fearful, obsessive tendencies or neuroses because they were so psychologically advanced. If they were afraid in their dreams, they would discuss it in depth with each other.

Confronting the Nightmare

When a Senoi child was frightened in a dream, he was advised to confront the fear. And, he was encouraged to call on dream friends to help him. If he was attacked in the dream, he was required to retaliate. Only then, they believed, would his attacker leave him alone.

"To confront and conquer danger," writes Patricia Garfield in her book *Creative Dreaming*, "is the most important rule in the Senoi system of dream control." Luckily, some of us stumble on this rule without ever having heard about the Senoi.

After a woman was assaulted, she repeatedly had dreams in which the attacker was chasing her. Finally, in the following dream, she seized control of the situation. This dream is titled "The Attacker":

The scene is the same as in the other dreams, the man chasing me down a dark alley between a pair of brownstone buildings. I'm so terrified, the inside of my mouth is bone dry. I can see the end of the alley just ahead, can see lights, traffic, but I know I'm not going to make it.

So I suddenly stop, turn, and demand that he leave me alone. He looks at me for a long moment, then holds out his hand. I can see something in his palm, but I don't want to approach him to take it. I tell him to drop it on the ground and he does. Then he walks away from me, whistling.

When he's gone, I walk over to where he was standing and find a beautiful, pink shell—the object he dropped. It has my name on it. I've never had the dream since.

The woman interpreted the shell as a womb, which serves as a protective shelter for a fetus. In this dream, the shell was a symbol of protection, which the woman had gained for herself. As in this case, the key is to take control of your nightmares. With practice, it can be done with great success. You will learn how to do this in Chapter 2.

CHAPTER 2

CONTROLLING YOUR NIGHTMARE

As you learned in the last chapter, bad dreams often reveal certain fears or anxieties that you might not have been aware of consciously. Analyzing those dreams and resolving those real-life issues can go a long way toward "de-fanging" your nightmares (maybe literally, if you're dreaming of toothy monsters).

But you can take an extra step, beyond fighting your nightmares after you've awakened. In this chapter, you will learn about a strategy called lucid dreaming. A lucid dream is one in which you're aware that you're dreaming. It may begin as a normal dream, but at some point you wake up inside the dream. Then, depending on your skill, you can manipulate the action in the dream and mold it, second by second.

Once you've mastered the skill of lucid dreaming, you'll be able to take control of your nightmares and shape them to your own desires. The confidence and authority you will feel from this process will cross over into your waking life, allowing you to take action against whatever factors were leading to your bad dreams in the first place. With a combination of lucid dreaming and dream analysis, you can banish nightmares for good.

An Introduction to Lucid Dreaming

For years, lucid dreaming was primarily the domain of parapsychologists—a critical factor in discouraging mainstream scientists from studying it. But in recent years, lucid dreaming has become a hot topic of study. Stephen LaBerge, a pioneer of lucid dreaming research, attributes this surge of interest, in part, to several landmark books.

In 1968, an English parapsychologist named Celia Green published *Lucid Dreams*. Her book included the most comprehensive overview of the literature available on the subject up to that time. During the 1970s, Ann Faraday, author of *The Dream Game*, and Patricia Garfield, author of *Creative Dreaming*, were instrumental in kindling popular interest in the subject. Even though serious scientific research on lucid dreaming didn't take place until the 1970s, it has been recognized for centuries.

Your First Lucid Dream

Very often, lucid dreams are first experienced accidentally. Without making any special preparations, you suddenly realize you are awake and still dreaming. If you're lucky, the experience will last for more than a few seconds.

For some people, lucidity may arise for the first time from a nightmare. But for most dreamers, LaBerge says, lucidity happens when you recognize some glaring inconsistency or bizarre factor in your dream. A first-time experience may also be triggered when you realize your dream is very familiar—that you've dreamed it before. LaBerge calls this entry into a lucid dream "*déjà rêve.*"

The technical term for this sort of lucid dream is "dream-induced lucid dreams" (DILD) and it is the most common way that people experience lucid dreams. Nearly everyone at some stage in life has experienced a lucid dream—waking up and being aware that you are still in a dream. The percentage of people who consistently experience this type of dream is relatively small. Approximately 20 percent have lucid dreams on a regular basis, meaning they have one or more a month.

Lucid dreams are usually initiated during the REM sleep stage, a period of deep sleep when a person's eyes begin to move rapidly under her eyelids. During a normal night of sleep, the REM stage will be experienced three or four times with the most intense REM close to the end of the total sleep period. Each time that REM occurs, there is the opportunity for a DILD to take place. Above all, remember to stay positive and resolved to develop your lucid dream experiences.

Keep a Dream Journal

Unless you are an experienced lucid dreamer, chances are that any lucid dreams you may have experienced were DILDs or dreams that you consciously knew were happening even though you knew you were still sleeping. It may be hard to remember whether or not some of your dreams were actually lucid. Dream experiences have a tendency to disappear from the conscious mind over time. In fact, some fade from memory as soon as the night or sleep period is over. Having a written record of your dreams will help you go back and refer to them at a later date. Dreams that do not make sense when you first experienced them may turn out to be more relevant to your life than you first thought.

Are You in Shape for Dreaming?

Being in shape means being willing to take care of yourself physically, mentally, and spiritually. In other words, eat healthy or at least be aware of what foods and drinks you are putting in your body. Alcohol, drugs (including sleeping pills), and some foods can affect sleep and dreams. If you keep a dream journal, you might want to include what you have consumed. The body also needs physical activity and many people say they sleep better when they get exercise. A healthy body can help to facilitate dreams. So can a mind that's relaxed and free of stress. A positive mental outlook can help promote a good night's sleep, too.

The longer your sleep period lasts the greater your chance of having more vivid and easily remembered dreams. As the sleep period winds on, you are more prone to having a longer REM cycle. That can mean longer-lasting dreams. Longer dreams may provide you with more substance to work with.

Your sleep cycle usually repeats itself several times a night, whether you are aware of it or not. Sometimes you have periods in your life when you dream a lot, but other times it seems as if you rarely dream. Your physical and mental condition may have something to do with that, and certain medications can also act as dream blockers.

Getting Enough Data

Some dream experts suggest recording at least 150 dreams and then looking for patterns and similarities. Chances are, you'll find many recurring themes and images to give you a clue into your hidden problems!

When you put together your dream journal, write a section about your dream history, at least what you can remember of it. As you go through this process, the goal is to prime your memory to help you recall dream experiences that you may have long forgotten. Ask yourself these questions—they may help facilitate your efforts:

- What is the earliest dream you can remember?
- What is the most recent dream you can remember?
- How many dreams can you remember having in the last month?
- Do any notable dreams stand out to you over the past year? Five years?
- Was there any time in your life when you experienced intense dream periods?
- Can you see themes or patterns related to your dreams?
- What are the most meaningful dreams you have had?
- Can you remember any lucid dreams?
- How often do you experience lucid dreams?
- Is there a pattern to your lucid dreams?
- Do you think that perhaps your dreams are being presented to you for guidance and understanding?
- Is there a greater meaning, something that science might not accept?
- Up to this time in your life, have your dreams, and particularly lucid dreams, been random?

Hopefully, these questions will help you begin to understand the nature of your dreams. You are the judge of whether your dreams are random or not, and especially your lucid dreams.

Recognizing the Dream

"Reality testing," a reasoning process normally delegated to the waking brain, is a way to distinguish lucid dreams from other kinds of dreams. With practice, you won't even have to ask if you're dreaming. Once you recognize some anomaly or bizarre event in the dream, your realization will be instantaneous.

In the following example, Anita's recurring dream about a Gothic house triggered a lucid dream. This dream is called "Gothic House as Launchpad":

> *As soon as I stepped into the house this time, I recognized it. I knew it was the Gothic house of my recurring dream, the place I had explored countless times in the past.*
>
> *With this realization, the dream turned lucid. I found myself in a sunlit living room, an immense and beautifully furnished room that I hadn't been in before. Just to make sure I was actually lucid, I leaped into the air to see if I could fly and I did! My astonishment was so great, I woke up.*

Am I Dreaming?

The most important part of inducing a lucid dream is to constantly ask yourself "Am I dreaming?" Ask yourself this question over and over, even if you are obviously awake. Sometimes our dreams are so incredibly lucid that we think we're awake when we are actually entering a dream state.

How do you prove to yourself that you are actually having a lucid dream? A process called a reality check can help you realize that you are, in fact, consciously aware and in control of your lucid dream. Your reality check will become part of your dream intentions as you expand your dream consciousness.

A reality check starts with doing a repetitive exercise when you are awake. To create a habit, you begin with consciously doing something. Eventually, as you practice the repetition of the exercise, it will become a part of your unconsciousness and be recalled to your consciousness when something reminds it to do so.

Here are three exercises you can practice several times a day to help you become aware of what to look for in a dream to prove you are really having a lucid dream:

- **Mirror test:** Every time you look at yourself in the mirror, make a mental note of how clear your reflected image is. Remind yourself that this is the real way that your image is reflected, and it will reflect the same way every time you observe yourself when you are awake. Suggest to yourself that when you dream, you will be able to observe yourself in a mirror. In a dream, your reflection will appear out of focus or somehow be different, proving to yourself that you are having a dream.

- **Wristwatch test:** Do this exercise several times a day. Look at the watch, note the time, look away for a brief moment, and then look back again. The time will look the same except for a few seconds. Tell yourself that this is real, and suggest to yourself that you will see your watch when you realize you are dreaming. When you look away and then look back at your watch in your dream, the time will be different, proving to you that you are dreaming.

- **Breath test:** Try to hold your nose while pressing your tongue on the roof of your mouth, covering the opening where air from your nose can enter your mouth. You will be unable to breathe. Remind yourself that you know this is real. Do this exercise several times a day. When you become aware you are dreaming, do the same exercise, and you will be able to breathe normally.

Lucid dream researchers have found that observations made in real life do not appear the same way in a dream, as in the watch example just described. If you look at your feet and then look away in a dream, when you look back again the ground will be different or you might be wearing different shoes.

You are also free to create your own reality checks. Again, it comes down to how you intend to prove to yourself that you are consciously aware that you are dreaming.

Every dream you are able to remember and record helps you increase your conscious awareness. It might take a few nights before you start achieving consistent results, but your ability to recognize that you are having a dream and being able to remember it will become a habit. After a while, it becomes a normal nightly routine.

Making It Happen

Wouldn't it be nice to be able to go to sleep knowing you were going to have an incredible lucid dream experience? Today, thanks to the work of Stephen LaBerge and others, you can learn to do just that. That said, it is good to remember that each of us experiences all dreams, including lucid dreams, differently than anyone else. One of the reasons for this is your different mental makeup. It all relates to how you imagine in your mind.

It's one thing to randomly find yourself dreaming lucidly, but quite another to teach yourself to do so. If you have never awakened inside a dream and would like to sample the experience, or if you've spontaneously entered a lucid dream in the past and would like to further explore this region of dreaming, there are various methods you can try to induce lucidity.

The best times to enter a lucid dream are just as you fall asleep or as you awaken after a night's sleep. If you fall asleep easily and quickly, with practice you can enter a lucid dream within minutes of lying down. LaBerge suggests using a counting method: "One, I'm dreaming. Two, I'm dreaming . . ." Once you reach a certain number, you'll say it aloud and will actually be dreaming.

Alternately, as you are falling asleep, focus on one particular thing—a visualization, your breath or heartbeat, how your body feels, or whatever you choose. "If you keep the mind sufficiently active while the tendency to enter REM sleep is strong," writes LaBerge, "you feel your body fall asleep but you, that is to say, your consciousness, remains awake." You may also find that a lucid state is easier to obtain after you've slept a while.

Why Is It so Important to Have a Lucid Dream?

Lucid dreams give us control over our waking lives. If we learn to recognize our wishes, hopes, and fears, and then how to restructure the "plot" of our dreams, we can effectively steer ourselves toward success on all fronts, waking and sleeping.

The In-Between State

Because your longest period of REM sleep is near morning, try not to open your eyes when you wake. Lie quietly and let your dream images surround and flow through you. Afterward, turn over on your side or change positions. The act of moving may allow you to think of yourself as awake as well as dreaming.

Developing a Sleep Routine

In *The Nature of Personal Reality*, Seth, a personality spoken through a medium, discusses the value of sleeping in four- or six-hour blocks instead of the usual eight-hour block that is customary in Western culture.

By following such a sleep routine, "there are not the great artificial divisions created between the two states of consciousness. The conscious mind is better able to remember and assimilate its dreaming experience, and in the dream the self can use the waking experience more efficiently."

Without ever mentioning the term "lucid dreaming," Seth says that by following this particular sleep routine, it becomes obvious that "the individual sense of identity can be retained in the dream state. When you find yourself as alert, responsive, and intellectual in the dream state as you are in waking life, it becomes impossible to operate within the old framework."

It's interesting to note that parapsychological writer Robert Monroe followed a sleep routine similar to what Seth describes. He frequently mentioned sleeping for "two cycles," a reference to two dream cycles of about four hours each. Jane Roberts, the writer and medium through whom the personality known as Seth spoke, and her husband also followed Seth's suggestions. They slept for six hours a night, with a half-hour nap in the afternoon, as needed.

Establishing Your Sleep Need

To develop a sleep routine, first determine how many hours of sleep you need—whether it's seven or eight or even nine. If the answer is seven, for example, try a six-hour block of sleep at night and an hour nap in the afternoon or right before dinner. Try several different combinations, and choose the one that works best for you. This routine is dependent on a flexible work schedule that lets you nap at some time during the day. If your schedule won't allow it, then try the routine on weekends or vacations, when your time is your own.

By stimulating your mind to focus on the real issues in your life, you can intensify the state of lucid dreaming. The following exercise can help you do this. For this exercise, list five fears or limitations you would like to overcome. Also list five goals you would like to achieve in the next three months, in six months, and in the next year. Create a game plan for incorporating these challenges and goals into your lucid dreaming program, and then put them into action. List these things:

- Five fears or limitations you would like to overcome
  1. _____
  2. _____
  3. _____
  4. _____
  5. _____

- Your plan for overcoming these limitations

  _____
  _____
  _____
  _____
  _____

- Five goals you would like to achieve in the next three months
  1. _____
  2. _____
  3. _____
  4. _____
  5. _____

- Your plan for achieving these goals

  _____
  _____
  _____
  _____
  _____

- Five goals you would like to achieve in the next six months

  1. _____
  2. _____
  3. _____
  4. _____
  5. _____

- Your plan for achieving these goals

  _____
  _____
  _____
  _____
  _____

Intent Is Everything

Your intention to explore the world of lucid dreaming is vital in triggering such a dream. When Stephen LaBerge was just beginning his research, he realized that as he clarified his intent to remember, the number of his lucid dreams increased dramatically. "Lucid dreaming rarely occurs without our intending it, which means having the mental set to recognize when we are dreaming; thus, intention forms a part of any deliberate effort to induce lucid dreams."

Malcolm Godwin, author of *The Lucid Dreamer: A Waking Guide for the Traveler Between Worlds,* notes that the method advocated by the tenth-century Tibetan master Atisha creates a similar effect: *Think that all phenomena are like dreams.* "For in continually thinking that everything is a dream during the day, that mind-set begins to appear in your nightly dreams, and suddenly you will start to experience yourself both deeply asleep and yet fully awake at the same moment."

As you'll see when you use lucid dreaming to control your nightmare, setting out the right intentions will be key to your success.

LaBerge suggests that you set memory targets during the day as a way of training your mind to wake up during a dream. In this method, you select objects or even sounds as triggers. For example, if you select two targets, the sound of a dog barking and the sight of a red car, you will note that you've found a target whenever you hear a bark or see the appointed vehicle. Once you've perfected your ability to remember and locate targets, you'll be able to use La Berge's lucid dreaming technique, described later in this chapter.

You may want to train your waking memory by giving yourself four specific targets each day. Memorize the day's targets. Record your successes. Every time you find one of the targets, write it down, and remember to ask yourself if you're dreaming. Keep track of how many targets you hit each day. If, at the end of the week, you've missed most of the targets, then continue the exercise for another week. Record the following:

- Day One Targets:

  _____

  _____

  _____

  _____

- Day One Hits:

  _____

  _____

  _____

  _____

- Day Two Targets:

  _____

  _____

  _____

  _____

- Day Two Hits:

  _____

  _____

  _____

  _____

Continue this exercise for five days and then examine your success rate. Did you find more targets as time went on? Did you get worse at the exercise? How did your strategy change?

LaBerge's MILD Technique

If you can't remember to do something when you're awake, you probably won't be able to remember to do it when you're asleep. But if you're successful with your target exercise, you should also be able to use LaBerge's MILD technique. Outlined in his book, *Exploring the World of Lucid Dreaming*, MILD stands for "Mnemonic Induction of Lucid Dreaming." This technique has five basic steps:

1. **Set up dream recall.** Simply state your intention to wake up through the night and recall your dreams.
2. **Recall your dream.** When you wake from a dream, try to recall as many details as possible. Don't tell yourself you'll remember the dream in the morning; chances are it will be gone by then. Force yourself to write it down in your dream journal right away.

3. **Focus your intent.** While you're falling back to sleep, focus on your intention to recognize that you're dreaming. Mean what you say. Stay centered on this one thought. Remember, intention is everything!

4. **Visualize yourself becoming lucid.** The best way to do this is to see yourself back in the dream from which you've just awakened. This time, however, recognize that it's a dream. Look for something to tip you off that you're dreaming. For example, as you relive the dream, decide that you're going to fly. See yourself doing it, see yourself realizing that you're dreaming, and then continue reliving the dream.

5. **Repeat.** LaBerge recommends repeating steps 3 and 4 just to fix your intention in your mind.

Mirror, Mirror on the Wall

Malcolm Godwin offers another method of entering a lucid dream that is a variation on an Eastern meditation technique known as *tratak*. Before going to sleep, sit comfortably in front of a mirror for about half an hour. Place a lighted candle nearby to illuminate your face, and stare steadily at your reflected image without blinking for as long as you can. The face in the mirror will start changing quite dramatically, like a series of wavering masks. Godwin notes that many practitioners believe these masks are images of our past lives.

As you continue to gaze into the mirror, *intend* to dream that night. Watch the changing faces for a while longer, and then ask to see your real face. "Meditators claim that in waking life the image in the mirror disappears altogether," Godwin says. "In lucid dreams prepare to be even more surprised."

No matter what method you use to reach the world of lucid dreams, once you become successful, the benefits are enormous. You can overcome your fears by directly confronting them in your lucid dreams. You can increase your self-knowledge, which expands your awareness. By consciously facing danger in your dreams, you develop self-confidence, which spills over into your everyday life. And you can solve problems in the dream state that will benefit your waking life. Try as many methods as it takes until you master the art of lucid dreaming.

Help Resolve Nightmares Through Lucid Dreaming

Nightmares can happen at any time. Think how great it would be to be able to change any of your bad dreams into pleasant ones. You can, through lucid dreaming. You can develop a technique to become aware that you are having a nightmare or even when you wake up from one. This technique will help you be ready to face and change your negative dreams.

In this section you will find out how to use your sources of belief and faith, including your guides or angels, to protect and watch over you as you use lucid dreaming to change your nightmares. You will have the opportunity to try an altered-state lucid dream trance to help resolve past-life-related nightmares as well as an exercise to keep nightmares out of your dreams.

Repetitious Nightmares

Most people experience nightmares at least occasionally, but you may find yourself facing nightmares with the same theme that repeats over and over, sometimes night after night. For people who suffer from nightmares, every night is often filled with anxiety or terror, which leaves them feeling exhausted the next day from lack of a good night's sleep.

Perhaps you have a child or know one who has a lot of nightmares. You may have had them yourself when you were young. It is hard to explain to children that what they are dreaming is not real. Their disrupted sleep can be just as hard on you. You may have felt the anxiety of wanting a child to feel safe and unafraid, or you may have had your own night's rest disturbed by a frightened child.

Setting Intentions for the Lucid Dream

Here are two specific sets of intentions to help you prepare for a lucid dream that changes a nightmare or any type of negative dream. The first set of intentions helps you resolve a repetitive nightmare. This can be done through the usual lucid dreaming techniques or through an altered state of consciousness lucid-dream trance.

If you are suffering from nightmares, have you kept an account of them in your dream journal? Asking yourself these questions may help you to better understand your nightmare pattern.

- *How often do you experience nightmares?* Every night, once a week, once a month, certain times of the year, or just randomly? Even if you have not kept a record of when they occur, you may be able to recall some approximate times over the last year or more.
- *Is there a pattern of events or other situations or conditions that precede a nightmare?* What was going on in your life before your nightmare? Was there additional stress? What did you eat, drink, read, watch on TV? Who did you talk to? Were they friends, relatives, adversaries? How is your general health? What medicine are you taking, drugs or homeopathic remedies? Was anything special happening at work or home?
- *Can you identify when your nightmares first started?* How long ago? How old were you? What happened in your life just before the first one?
- *Do you have any medical issues that might contribute to a nightmare?* Do you have sleep apnea? If you are

struggling to get air when you are sleeping, it may cause you to experience a nightmare.

- *Could your sleep position contribute to your nightmares?* Simply changing your sleep position may help eliminate nightmares.

Understanding how you experience your nightmares can help you set clearer intentions. Some of your nightmares may not be resolved through lucid dreaming. Nightmares that are caused by food, medications, or other stimulants that speed up your pulse rate are created by an actual physical condition.

Intentions for Random Nightmares

Not all nightmares are repetitive. Sometimes we can't know exactly what we are going to face before we go to sleep. This second set of intentions is designed to help you not only be consciously aware of when you are experiencing a nightmare or negative dream, but also how to change those types of dreams into positive ones. You can prepare for these experiences as you would prepare for the possibility of a situation that may or may not happen in your waking life. You might think of it as defensive driving in your sleep.

These intentions can be used to work with random nightmares or ones that may have a common theme. You can answer the same questions regarding repetitive nightmares to help you understand what you have been experiencing. However, the intentions you are now creating are for nightmares that could happen at any time.

INTENTION EXERCISE

Try writing a lucid dream intention mantra that can become your mantra to attract lucid dreams, so that you'll be able to deal with unexpected nightmares when they come.

These are the key points you should cover when writing your intentions:

- **Goal.** "Tonight, I look forward to experiencing a lucid dream."
- **Awareness.** "I will stay consciously aware as I experience my lucid dream."
- **Reality check.** "I know it is real when the clock has a different time when I look away and look back."
- **Remember.** "When I wake up, I will remember every detail of my dream."

Let's see how you could take those four points and create a mantra; the goal is to combine and create a single sentence that is easy to remember. "Tonight I will be consciously aware as I drift into my lucid dream, will know it is real when I look at the clock face, and will fully remember my dream afterward."

Now you should try putting together your intentions to create a mantra that is right for you.

Knowing You're Not Alone

Another very positive factor that you can bring into play when you experience a nightmare is your faith or belief in a higher power—in something or someone that watches over you. It is not easy facing the world alone, especially in the dark of a nightmare. Just knowing in your mind that you are not alone as you face and change your nightmares and negative dreams can be of great comfort. There are a couple ways that you can incorporate your belief to help you making positive changes through a lucid dream.

Once you are confident that there really is something with you—for instance, an angel, deity, spirit guide, your higher self—you can establish an intention that your conscious mind will always know that you are not alone. As you repeat this to yourself, feel love and gratitude that you are being watched over, not only while you sleep but at all times. Regardless of what is going on in your life, faith can be a positive force that helps you carry the weight of life so you don't have to feel the need to hold up the whole world.

Protective Intentions

A prayer can be an intention. Wording your prayers with gratitude and love can help strengthen your intention. Remember, what you get out of your intention depends on what you put into it. You get back what you send out. Knowing when you wake up in the middle of the night that you are surrounded by something positive and protective may help you find peace of mind.

You can use your protection intention many times a day. It could be when you are traveling, working, or in the shower. You can use your intention as a mantra. The more you consciously repeat it, the more powerful it will become in your unconscious mind. When you need it, it will automatically come into your conscious mind.

A Gratitude Protection Intention

Thank you for being with me and watching over me as I sleep. Thank you for helping me face and change any nightmares that I may encounter in my dreams.

You can also set an intention that you will be consciously aware of not being alone when you encounter a negative dream or a nightmare. You can intend that you will test the reality of the dream, surround yourself with the protective elements that go with you, change the nightmare, and create a positive outcome. You can intend that when you wake up after having experienced a nightmare, you will put yourself back into it, surrounded by your protective team of helpers and guardians. Once you prove to yourself that you are dreaming and you feel safe with the assistance of your protectors, you can go about changing the negative dream or nightmare.

Changing the Nightmare Through Lucid Dreaming

You can now set about changing a nightmare through your lucid dreaming because you know the dream isn't real and that you are not alone. Here are some ideas to consider, ways that you could make changes during a lucid dream. It really boils down to what approach works for you, what is comfortable and feels right. By thinking about what you might use and imagining what the positive results would be, you are bringing your intentions into your conscious awareness.

- You can choose to become invisible and watch what's happening, knowing you can't be seen.
- You can contact helpers to get rid of the bad parts in the dream.
- You can create a protective shield that blocks the nightmare from returning.
- You can journey back in time to the beginning of the nightmare and change the beginning by creating a different dream.
- You can shrink giants down to nothing or blast the bad guys with powerful laser beams.

- If you wake up in a war, you can go back in time and create peace.
- If you are starving, you can create an abundance of food.
- If you are cold, you can move the dream to a pleasant, warm place.
- If you wake up in another time period, you can come back to the present.
- If you are dying, you can go back before the scene began to change the outcome and the negative situation.

Dealing with Childhood Nightmares

Perhaps you have a child or know one who's plagued by nightmares and could benefit by knowing that she can change them so that they won't come back. Focus on the child's positive images before looking at the negative ones. First, identify what is safe and protective to the child. It may be a parent, friend, stuffed toy, or something known only to the child's mind. It doesn't make any difference what she chooses, so long as she associates a strong feeling of protection with it. Next, have her imagine her superhero being with her at all times, watching over and protecting her, especially when she dreams. Suggest to the child that she is now always safe and protected and free from nightmares.

If you are psychically dreaming of something negative in the future, you can ask your team of helpers to change the results by taking the right actions during your waking life to help change the negative outcomes shown in your psychic dreams. You may also intend that you only dream psychically of things on which you can have a positive effect.

Using Guided Altered-State Nightmare Resolution

You can also use altered states of consciousness to produce lucid dream experiences. The object is to hold onto conscious awareness and move directly into a dream experience using a trance state sleep rather than actually drifting off to sleep. Those who are most successful with this technique are often people who are used to practicing powerful mind-focusing exercises such as meditation, yoga, or self-hypnosis.

Not everyone is capable of entering into a deep state of focus. Some people just have a natural awareness of their environment and have trouble letting go or focusing on a single thought or purpose. For this type of individual, something will usually pull their focus away from entering into a deep altered state of consciousness. People are products of their environment, and for those who have learned to be highly vigilant of their surroundings, focusing on one thought may be difficult.

CONSCIOUS AWARENESS

As you consciously move from your waking state to your trance sleep-like state, you progress through a series of steps, each one moving you deeper into a trance or altered state of consciousness. In order to move on to the next step, it is necessary to accept the reality of the last step. If you suggest to yourself that your muscles are relaxing, then you need to feel that your muscles are actually relaxing. As you accept these suggestions, you are also maintaining a conscious awareness of what you are experiencing as you experience it.

The Trance Tracer

Hypnotist Harry Arons developed a method of testing how deep into a trance his subjects would go. This technique, known as the Arons Depth Scale, classifies hypnosis subjects into six different categories of trance. Level one is a light trance, like daydreaming, and level six is the deepest trance, where the subject has no conscious awareness.

One of the advantages of staying consciously aware through your induction process is that it may help you set up specific goals during a lucid dream experience. For instance, you may want to work on self-improvement or practice and hone a skill while you are lucid dreaming.

The key is patience. The goal is to help you determine and develop the right lucid dreaming technique for you.

SELF-INDUCED ALTERED STATES

To begin to enter a self-induced altered state of consciousness, simply focus on your breathing. Take a deep breath that is comfortable for you, and slowly exhale. As your breathing slows down, your mind may begin to empty. When you focus on a lot of thoughts, you may be concentrating so hard on what you are thinking that you forget to breathe. Shallow breathing can deprive the body of oxygen and make it hard to focus on just relaxing.

Today's stress brings out our natural instinct of flight or fight. Early man developed this ability for survival. However, it can be detrimental to your health if your constant focus is centered on something that is stressful. Our stress warning system was developed for short-term situations, not the long-term conditions often faced today.

That is why it is important to remember to breathe. One of your first goals or intentions when you are entering into an altered state of consciousness should be to begin to relax when you start focusing on your breathing. In fact, as you learn to relax, you will probably find that you enjoy it. Once you have learned to expect the enjoyment, just the thought of deeper breathing will help you anticipate the positive experience you will have when you are doing it.

FUTURE PACING

There is a term in hypnosis called future pacing. What it means is that you are suggesting to yourself that you will have a certain experience when a specific action begins. By expecting to experience the positive benefit of relaxing when you start to focus on your breathing, you are giving yourself an expectation of what will happen to you when the process begins. Future pacing helps you narrow your focus on deepening your altered state of consciousness.

By using future pacing when you are writing your self-induction script, you will create stronger intentions to help you focus. Once you get used to the concept of future pacing, it will become easier and easier for you to enter into a self-induced altered state of focus. In fact, once you become accustomed to the process and have created a method that is right for you, the moment you begin to focus on your breathing, you enter into a deeper altered state of consciousness in a shorter amount of time. What you will be doing is creating an expectation that the next time you start a self-induced altered state induction, you will automatically slip easily back into your trance.

SELF-GUIDED NIGHTMARE RESOLUTION IN AN ALTERED STATE.

A guided altered state of consciousness lucid-dream trance can prove to be a valuable technique in helping someone eliminate nightmares that have plagued him for a long time. This method is especially good for a repetitious nightmare that may be connected to one or more past lives. You could create your own guided imagery to guide you through your lucid dreamlike trance process. You will experience your trance differently than anyone else because of the way you process images in your mind's eye. You may be able to watch the process like a dream movie, experience the dream trance while it is taking place, or both.

If your nightmare is connected to another time period, the goal is to go back and understand what happened. Then, either change the outcome or go back before the negativity started. When you find something positive in the past, you can connect to that character or part of your soul and bring positive healing and resolution to the outcome.

The Fun of Lucid Dreaming

Once you've become proficient at lucid dreaming, you can use it for many things besides resolving your nightmares. For some people, lucid dreams offer a way to have adventures they would never be able to enjoy during their normal waking lives. They can take a rocket ship to the moon or dive to the depths of an ocean. They can go back in time to experience what it was like to live in another period of history. They can journey into the future and experience what it will be like in years to come.

Here is a past-life, nightmare-resolution, lucid-dream trance exercise you can try. You can use it as is, change it, or create an entirely different one:

Take a few moments and get comfortable in the place where you would like to try this exercise. Take a deep breath and slowly exhale. Continue to do this as you feel gratitude and love in your heart for the protective team that surrounds and helps you to resolve and heal issues from your past that surface in your nightmares.

Let yourself feel safe and protected as your eyes go out of focus. Feel your muscles begin to relax, starting at the top of your head and working your way downward to your feet. Remind yourself of your intentions to experience a lucid-dream trance that lets you change, heal, and resolve your nightmares in a positive way.

When you are ready, begin to count yourself downward from five to zero, suggesting to yourself as you do that you will remain consciously aware as you drift into your lucid-dream trance. You will be watched over and protected by your team the whole time you are in your lucid-dream trance as well as before and afterward.

Suggest to yourself that when you reach zero, you will recall an image in your mind's eye of a past nightmare, and you will be able to watch the image as a movie in your mind. You will also be able to step in and out of the images to learn the reason for the nightmares.

As you slowly count down, remind yourself of your intentions, repeating your suggestions in between each count. Five (pause). Four (pause). Three (pause). Two (pause). One (pause). Zero (pause). When you get to zero, feel yourself surrounded by your protective team. Focus on the images that come into your mind's eye.

Now go to a place before the nightmare starts. It could be a happy time in the life of the character that you experienced in the nightmare. See this character. Look through his eyes as if you were the person you saw in your mind's eye. What do his clothes look and feel like? How does his hair look and feel? What does he have on his feet? What is the temperature and time of day? What is the character's mood? Are there any sounds, smells, or tastes? What is happening around this person?

Watch the images as if you were watching a movie, as they move forward to when the cause of your nightmare began. Did the character in your mind's eye die then? If not, move forward to when this person died and know his last thoughts without experiencing any of this physically.

You now have the option of changing the scene or going back to a happier time period and connecting that experience to you as you are now. Bring healing over the negative outcome with your heart power of love and gratitude. For a moment, move forward in your life to see how what you've learned can help you in the future.

Now go back in time and check to see if there were other episodes that are contributing to your nightmares. If you find more, do the same exercise until they have all been resolved. Dream your way forward again and experience sleep without any nightmares. As you count slowly back from zero to five, suggest to yourself that you will continue to remember that you have resolved and healed your old nightmare issues. Feel gratitude and love as you come back to the surface of your conscious mind, fully aware of where you are and of feeling relaxed and positive.

Resolving Nightmares in a Guided Altered State

It is possible for someone else, such as a hypnotist, to guide you into an altered state of consciousness that creates the experience of a lucid dream. Just as you might be a natural lucid dreamer without any type of training who knows how to consciously interact with your dreams, you might also naturally enter into deep hypnotic states. It all depends on your ability to focus on your imagination. The more real your images become the deeper you will go into a trance.

A hypnotist is actually a facilitator to help guide you into an altered state of consciousness. You are creating the experience yourself with the suggestions of the facilitator. It is possible for you to facilitate your own altered state of consciousness (as detailed above), but it may be easier for someone else to do that for you. The benefit of working with someone else is that you do not have to remain as alert as you would if you were doing it all by yourself.

THE POWER OF SUGGESTION

A facilitator can use the power of suggestion coupled with future pacing to help induce you into a lucid dream experience. Once you have entered into a deep altered state of focus, the suggestion can be made to you that you will now find yourself in a lucid dream, fully aware and able to move throughout the dream and make changes if you wish. The facilitator can suggest that you dream about a predetermined topic or that you will experience just the right lucid dream for you at that time.

"All Hypnosis Is Self-Hypnosis"

That means it is the individual who creates a trance, not the facilitator or hypnotist. Another word for hypnotist is "operator," and his role is to offer suggestions that help influence the trance that the individual creates. If the individual resists the suggestions, they do not enter into a trance.

Once you know what a lucid dream is, the facilitator can suggest that you will experience a lucid dream and be fully able to be consciously aware of and interact with it while you are in your altered state of consciousness trance. It can also be suggested that when you come back to full consciousness, you will remember all the details of the lucid dream you experienced. You may not be able to determine whether you had a lucid dream or were in a hypnotic trance, but it could be said that you experienced a lucid dream while you were in an altered state of consciousness.

BENEFITS OF A FACILITATED DREAM TRANCE

There is one major benefit to a facilitated altered-state lucid dream trance: the facilitator can also interact with the lucid dream. You can provide a running commentary on what is taking place while it is happening, and he can offer suggestions that might help provide much more information on the lucid dream than you would normally bring back when you come out of your dream state.

A trained facilitator or hypnotist has the ability to recognize what you may need to experience in a lucid dream trance. He can set up scenarios for the dream and guide you through your experiences. He can also help you stay in a lucid dream trance where you, by yourself, might come back to the surface of your mind before you got the full benefit of the lucid dream experience. Of course, you do not have to have a specific goal to have a lucid dream-trance experience. You can enter a lucid dream trance just for the experience itself.

SPEAKING FROM AN ALTERED STATE OF CONSCIOUSNESS LUCID DREAM

As long as there is a connection between the facilitator and the subject, the subject will be able to respond to the facilitator's communication. There is a point after the subject has been induced into an altered state of consciousness or hypnagogic state when interaction with the subject ceases and she drifts off into sleep. Some people listen to recorded voice suggestions at night to help them sleep. The last suggestion she hears might be something like, "As this recording ends, you will drift off into a restful, relaxing sleep."

Probing for Past Lives

Skilled past-life facilitators can create altered states of consciousness that guide the subject into memories of past lives and move them around in the life to understand how that life may have impacted their current life. This experience can help resolve issues that can create positive changes in the subject's life.

When a hypnotized subject has been given the suggestion that she is having a lucid dream experience, she still maintains contact with the facilitator of the session. She can be asked questions about what she is experiencing and hear suggestions to change the images in the dream. Just as in any other lucid dream, the subject can be instructed to tell herself that her experience isn't real, and therefore she can change it any way she wants. Because the facilitator is monitoring or in control of what the subject is dreaming, he can suggest the outcomes that are best for the subject.

A facilitated altered-state lucid dream is a very valuable experience for someone dealing with nightmares. With DILD, the subject would prepare for a lucid dream experience and then be ready for it when it happens. In a facilitated altered state, a highly suggestible subject can have a lucid dream experience on the first attempt that has a good chance of resolving the nightmare. In fact, a suggestion can be given to the subject at the end of the lucid dream imagery that they will not experience the nightmare again.

REMEMBERING THE EXPERIENCE

If you are in a deep altered state of consciousness, can you remember your experiences? The answer is yes, if you are given a suggestion that you will recall what went on while you were in the altered state. Some subjects that lose total contact with their conscious minds while in an altered state may have no memory of the events when they come back to full consciousness. Some will have partial memories with more details coming within a period of time, depending on the depth of the trance.

You should always be given positive suggestions as you come out of your altered state of consciousness. The facilitator might suggest:

When you come back to full conscious awareness, you will feel positive and relaxed. You will fully remember your lucid dream experiences without being affected by anything that may have seemed negative. You will understand how you were able to make any positive changes that may have been needed in your dream. You feel positive and relaxed and fully aware of your surroundings.

To Remember, to Forget

It can be suggested to a hypnotized subject that they will not remember anything they experienced when they wake from an altered state. That memory can easily be restored by another suggestion to remember. It can also be suggested that over the next few days the subject will remember more details as the information in the experience is processed.

The suggestions should be designed to be positive and supporting. The wording varies according to the lucid dream goals and experience. It is important to word them so that you will fully remember the lucid dream experience in a way that, if there were negative situations, you will not be impacted by anything you imagined during the dream.

Because you will be very focused on the facilitator's words, careful consideration needs to be given so that you will respond as intended.

You need a little time to adjust to your surroundings when you come out of an altered state. Perhaps you have had a dream that was so intense that when you woke you weren't sure where you were. This can be especially disconcerting when something causes you to wake up suddenly. The same thing is true when you come out of an altered state of consciousness.

Making Sure the Change Is Permanent

After your lucid-dream trance is over, suggest to yourself that you will continue to be surrounded by the love and support of your protective team wherever you go or whenever you dream in your sleep. Every day, remind yourself that you are grateful to be free of the old nightmares. Many times a day stop and take a breath and feel the positive energy that surrounds you.

Define what the nightmare used to be like in your mind's eye. Create a positive protective image through all five of your senses. Take a few moments and feel this image with gratitude and love.

Practice Makes Perfect

Practice makes perfect. The more you practice positive mind's-eye imagery that includes unconditional love and gratitude, the more it will become a part of your total self. Once the unconscious mind has absorbed the message of unconditional love and gratitude, you will recall and experience the message in your conscious mind, just as you intended to do.

Now bring back the negative image. Place a small positive image in the big negative one. Now push the positive one through the negative to push it away. Bring back the negative and repeat the process until there is no room for the negative image to return. Take a breath, exhale, and feel gratitude that you are now free from your old negative images and dreams. Doing this exercise once a day may help keep the nightmare "boogie man" away.

PART 2
Nightmare Dictionary

In order to banish your nightmares, you must first uncover their hidden meaning(s). Once you understand what your subconscious is trying to tell you, you'll be able to resolve your waking fear and anxieties, or even recognize warnings that you might not have caught. Keep this book on your nightstand, so that it's close by when you wake up after a bad dream. Then look through the dictionary to learn the significance behind the symbols, situations, and people in your nightmare.

A

Abandonment

Nightmares of being abandoned by a lover, friend, or family member suggest that this is something you fear in waking life. Childhood feelings of being left out often translate into abandonment dreams. In this case, you need to work on strengthening your self-esteem. You may have not spoken up for yourself in a difficult situation. In that case the dream might indicate that you have abandoned yourself, your principles, or values.

Abdomen

Seeing your abdomen in a nightmare suggests the gestation or digestion of a new idea or phase of your life. If your abdomen is swollen, the birth of a new project might be imminent.

Abduction

If you're abducted or kidnapped in your dream, it means you're feeling pressured to do or say something you don't believe in and don't want to do in waking life. Abduction dreams often stem from guilt concerning things you've done or are about to do that aren't typically in your character. If you witness someone else being abducted, it means you're not acting on the opportunities you've been given.

Abduction dreams can also indicate you feel someone else is unfairly receiving credit for your work.

Abnormality

If strangely formed things appear in your nightmare—a crooked mirror, a misshapen arm—don't be alarmed. One interpretation is that your mind might be open to new and unusual things. However, the bad dream could also be telling you something that appears "normal" is not what it seems. If you dream someone you know has an abnormality, your intuition could be cautioning you that the person is not who she appears to be.

Abortion

Dreaming of abortion is not usually literal. Many times, an abortion dream reflects the guilt you feel about doing something you shouldn't. The abortion in the dream is a warning to "abort" your actions and stop. The bad dream can indicate fears about a direction you are taking in your life. It may warn you that you have a tendency to stop out of fear and miss opportunities the new direction presents. Dreaming of an abortion might indicate a relationship has suddenly gone off course, or that your behavior or the other person's is killing some aspect of the relationship.

Absence

If have a bad dream in which someone is conspicuously absent, you may be looking within yourself for something or some quality that person possesses. This is a form of an anxiety dream, in which you are searching for important items in your life. What are you missing, either in your work situation, a relationship, or within yourself, that you need to be happy?

Abuse

If you dream of being abused, it's a sign you feel you're being taken advantage of in some way in your waking life. You feel powerless or helpless to protect yourself in a situation or relationship. You may also be receiving information from your subconscious that you are abusing some responsibility or gift you have been given.

Abyss

In the tarot, this is the place where faith is tested, the place from which the Fool leaps to discover his or her magic. No surprise, then, that a nightmare with an abyss can represent obstacles, uncertainty, and also fear—of the unknown, of failure, of your own capabilities, or whatever else is pressing on your mind. After all, the image of teetering over the edge of a cliff, chasm, precipice, or pit—images related to abysses—is one that is keenly chiseled into our collective consciousness. These notions all relate back to the fear of falling into a dangerous unknown or a depth of emptiness.

In a totally different sense, an abyss may represent fertility (the womb), and new beginnings. Play close attention to the context of the dream.

Accident

A car crash in a nightmare can be a literal warning—be careful in the coming weeks or months. However, vehicles in dreams often symbolize transitions in life. A car accident, particularly if you are driving in the dream, may indicate you feel the changes you are making in your life won't succeed. A skiing accident or crash while going very fast is an out-of-control release dream. It advises you to take hold of your life before things get more complicated. A plane crash usually indicates worrisome thoughts. Where are you experiencing worry or anxiety? Accidents at sea relate to your emotional nature—perhaps you feel your emotions have gone dangerously off course or you are on a collision course with someone important in your life. Most crash dreams are not precognitive, so first try to see what information the dream might be giving you about where you are going in your life, not just in everyday matters but on many levels.

Accusation

Accusations in a bad dream may be literal. Do you believe you've done something wrong? If you're accused, you may feel you're being judged or unfairly treated. The person judging you in these dreams is usually you. This dream could also reflect worries about how other people perceive you.

Ache

Aches or pains in your nightmares can be literal sensations coming from the physical body while you are sleeping. If the ache or pain seems severe in the dream, it might be time to get a checkup. If you actually feel the pain in the dream, you're probably half-lucid and feel the pain in waking life, as well. If the ache is imaginary, it could mean you are hurting emotionally in your waking life at this time. Often the body sends a message during a dream to alert you to something you may not be aware of in your waking life.

Acid

To dream of acid being poured on you signifies your anxiety levels are high right now. It may be time to take a break. If you dream of drinking acid, the dream is a metaphor that something is "eating you up." Figure out what's bothering you and fix it.

Addict/Addiction

If you dream someone is an addict or has an addiction, your nightmare may be alerting you to something that has not been revealed about someone you know. If you are the addict or addicted in the dream, your subconscious is letting you know you are obsessing about something to your detriment. You don't feel in control of whatever is happening in your life and seem helpless to control your need for the situation to continue.

Adultery

If you have a nightmare in which your partner is committing adultery, chances are you worry he could. But it doesn't necessarily mean he is unfaithful. In this case, use the dream as a jumping-off point to explore possible problems in the relationship. Adultery can just signify you are not being honest about your needs and feelings in a relationship. Make sure you communicate with your partner often to maintain closeness. If you are not in a relationship, think about where in your life you may be betraying your values.

Affliction

Dreaming that you have an affliction of some kind can mean you feel some part of you is unable to do what you want. Figure out what is holding you back. This nightmare rarely signifies an actual physical affliction.

Agate

Eye agate, traditionally used for protection from the "evil eye," represents the need for safety. If you have a nightmare in which agate features, it may be your subconscious telling you that you need protection.

Aggression

Aggression in a bad dream could be an emotional release dream of pent-up frustration or anger at a person or situation in your waking life—even at yourself. If you are not the aggressor in the dream, you might feel someone has control over you. Perhaps you feel weak and vulnerable. Think about where you are being pressured and by whom. If you're the aggressive one, you may harbor resentment against yourself or the person you're attacking. Usually, this type of dream signifies an emotional release of stresses built up during the day.

Airplane

If you dream you are on a plane that is going to crash, you are releasing fear in the dream state that you won't be safe or survive if you let go of your old way of seeing things.

Alarm

If you have a nightmare in which an alarm is ringing in warning, it indicates you have worries about some aspect of your life. Alarm clocks also sound each morning when it's time to rise and shine, so consider whether your dream is suggesting that you are in need of a "wakeup call" in some area of your life.

Alien

In a general sense, aliens in a nightmare can represent fear of the unknown. Pay attention to your feelings toward the aliens in your dreams, though. If you dream that you encounter people from outer space and you feel strange around them, then strange things may start to happen in your life.

Alligator

This symbol may suggest that you're being thick-skinned or insensitive to someone else. But be careful, an alligator may also signify danger.

Altar

An in-between place or bridge between the mundane and the eternal, an altar may represent the need to give or receive an offering. In ancient times, altars were places to make sacrifices and offerings, so this image has a longstanding link with such associations. Today, in contemporary times, altars remain places central to worship, where people gather to be in the presence of the Divine together, and to share and take part in things such Communion, in the case of Christianity, for example. Consider, therefore, if there's any connection in your dream to this sort of mingling.

For many people, houses of worship also serve as a reminder of repentance; thus, in dreams altars might provide a hint about not doing the wrong things.

Also, consider a play on words here: Is there anything that has been "altered" or is going to "alter" something in your life that is causing you concern?

Ambulance

Being in an ambulance most often indicates a release of anxiety and a desire to heal your emotional imbalance. You may be worrying over things that are out of your control. If you have a medical problem in the dream, though, it might be time to get a checkup. If you see someone else in an ambulance, you may have hidden guilt about hurting that person in some way. If you have been dealing with one crisis after another at home or work, everything can feel like an emergency! In that case, learn to ask for help.

Amputation

To have a nightmare about losing a limb might symbolically represent a sense of losing or severing some other part of yourself in a more abstract way. If someone else in your dream has had a leg or arm amputated, it is a reflection of something that person has been cut off from and, perhaps, something you might have taken away from or denied her.

Animals

Animals represent human beings' negative and positive qualities, and the wilder the animal, the more primitive the emotion. Animals also have very strong instincts; therefore, a dream of an animal might relate to your own instincts and intuition. Additionally, animals can signify various sides of your "animal" nature, and dreaming of animals in general implies an awakening of the tribal soul (humans are, after all, animals too). In dreams, animals can also represent a guardian spirit, wisdom, innocence, predatory tendencies, or sexuality, depending on the perceived nature of the animal. The characteristics you connect with the animal can be clues to the dream's meaning. An animal might additionally signify the physical body, or appear as a metaphor for an illness within the physical body.

Animals as Guides

Animals you encounter in your dreams can be symbolic or actual guides. Psychic Sylvia Browne calls them totems. She says that before a soul is reborn into this world again, it picks its protectors: a spirit guide, a totem (or animal guide), and angels who will help it through both dreams and waking life.

Aggressive animals warn either of danger in your life or denote a sense of feeling threatened. Dreaming of an animal being tamed brings a warning to control your primal nature (for instance, to curb your overly exuberant physical passion). If an animal is killed in your dream, some type of literal or figurative death is going on around you.

Ant

Ants suggest restlessness—in other words, feeling "antsy." They also signify small annoyances and irritations. Alternately, they may represent feelings of smallness or insignificance. If you dream of ants, consider the number of them present in the dream. Are you dreaming of a single ant, a colony, or a huge, swollen anthill?

If, in your dream, an ant is being crushed by a huge foot, ask yourself if you feel as if someone or something is squelching you. For example, is your industrious nature being stunted by someone in a place of authority, or is someone purposefully trying to undermine your job?

Anxiety

Anxiety is one of the most common nightmare experiences. Normally, anxieties in your waking life translate into your dreams in strange ways. Anxiety dreams do not need deep analysis. Let your subconscious work it out for you while you sleep on it. Just know you have released some of the anxiety that has built up during your day.

Appointment

A missed appointment signifies the same thing as a missed train, bus, or airplane. You've missed an opportunity or will miss one if you don't act soon. Figure out what that opportunity is, and put your best foot forward. If you have an appointment coming up and you dream you've missed it, you are just releasing anxiety about something that is important to you.

Apparition

An apparition can signify a message or warning. It can also be seen as communication with the dead. Alternately, you might feel that another person in a relationship is like an apparition—someone who is there, but not truly present.

Argument

If you have a bad dream in which you're arguing with someone, it could mean you fear intimacy with this person in waking life. On the other hand, it may also be that you've had an argument or sense an argument is soon to come. If you see two people arguing in your dream, it indicates you feel there is too much confusion around you right now. Lighten your load.

Ashes

Ashes are what's left of a substance after it's consumed by fire. Consider, therefore, if something in your life can be equated with remnants or residual leftovers, whether it be from a relationship, work situation, or anything else.

Additionally, ashes are a symbol of penance, as in the ashes smudged on the foreheads of Catholics on Ash Wednesday, at the start of Lent. Therefore, they might represent something you feel you need to account or make up for.

Further, consider the words commonly recited at funerals —"Ashes to ashes, dust to dust . . ."—which allude back to Genesis 3:19, a passage that describes human beings returning to the ground, and to dust, when we die. Taken in this light, it's easy to recognize ashes as a symbol of mortality in our culture's collective consciousness.

Be aware of your own attitude toward ashes, and how they figure in your bad dream. This will help you in analyzing and resolving the nightmare.

Athame

The ritual knife of Witchcraft, Wicca, and other neopagan practices, the athame represents the reality that tools are often double-edged and can be wielded to help or harm. This double-sided image could also apply to other situations—bear in mind the old "double-edged sword" cliché.

Attack

A nightmare involving an attack falls into the fear/anxiety category. Whether the dream attack occurs in a frightening, surreal, or supernatural situation, or in a gritty, realistic scenario, some key points apply. Attack dreams always express a feeling of vulnerability, uncertainty, and powerlessness. Keep in mind that your behavior and responses when being attacked in a dream are just as important as those of the person or thing that is attacking you. Are you weak and unable to retaliate, or do you maintain your composure and stand up to your attacker?

In the instance of being attacked, consider whether there is something in your life that you feel the need to fight back against or defend yourself from. If, on the other hand, you are the one doing the attacking in the dream, look at things from the opposite side of the spectrum and consider whether or not you are the one inadvertently keeping someone else down.

Attic

Whether or not you have a real attic in your home or grew up in a house with an attic, you might find yourself dreaming you are in an attic. Usually, the attic is the place of memories and family legacies. If you dream you are in the attic, you may be feeling nostalgic about times past, or you may be processing family patterns that are causing distress in your waking life.

The attic can also be the place of rediscovered treasures you didn't know you had. If you dream you find something unexpected in the attic, your subconscious is alerting you to gifts you have within yourself that you need to rediscover and express.

Perhaps you should take some part of yourself out of "storage" or dispose of things you are clinging to from your past. You may be exploring the realm of the higher self or seeking knowledge from a higher source in your dream.

Avalanche

Dreaming of an avalanche can signify a large obstacle in your path—something that might feel, perhaps, as if it's burying you. Keep in mind that avalanches have a cumulative effect: They pick up more snow, debris, and speed as they go along. Consequently, if you have a nightmare featuring an avalanche, consider whether there is a situation in your life that is "snowballing" in this way.

Ax

How is the ax used in your bad dream? If you're wielding it, it means that you are trying to chop a problem or situation down into manageable pieces. If the ax is aimed at you, you may fear someone is trying to take away important parts of who you are.

B

Back

When your back is turned, you are unaware of who or what might sneak up on you, and you can't see what's going on. Therefore, this symbol indicates a sense of vulnerability or lack of control. Your backbone is another associated element, and having a "backbone" (or not) figuratively implies a sense of courage, resolution, strength of character, determination, and strong will. Other related analogies include "backing off" or giving yourself space from a situation; being "stabbed in the back" or betrayed by someone; and the desire for "backup" or support.

Backward

If you dream you are walking, moving, or traveling backward in your dream—or slipping backwards—you feel you are covering old ground in some situation in your life. You may be slipping into old patterns of behavior, thinking, or emotional response.

Bad

Dreams in which you are being told you are bad relate to inner judgments you make about your own behavior or value. If you dream someone else is bad, you see in that person an aspect or quality of yourself that you feel is not healthy for you. If you feel bad in the dream, you might be feeling guilty or sorrowful about an action you have taken or failed to take that has, in some way, let you or others down.

Baldness

For a woman to have a nightmare about being bald indicates her fear of getting older or losing her femininity and appeal. For a man to dream he is bald signifies his fear of loss or a desire to come completely clean in a situation.

Barbs/Barbed wire

Barbed wire in a nightmare may indicate you feel confined or restricted in some area of your life. If you are trying to go somewhere and have to cross barbed wire, you might be in a life transition that you fear will be painful. If you cut yourself on a barb or barbed wire, you fear being emotionally hurt in a situation, possibly by someone's "barbed" tongue.

Basement

Dreaming of being in a basement might indicate that you are connecting with the subconscious mind. You might be unearthing something hidden in your past that you need to examine. A nightmare of a basement could also signify that your pleasure and prosperous possibilities might lessen or even develop into trouble.

Bat

Bats have an amazing ability to maneuver through dark places like caves with much agility in flight. Therefore, a dream of a bat suggests making your way through an uncertain situation successfully.

Digestion and Dreams

Certain food eaten too late in the day can contribute to dreams and nightmares. Alcohol or carbohydrates can turn to sugar and cause your heart rate to increase while you are sleeping. If this occurs during REM, chances are you will experience a nightmare and you will wake up with your heart pounding. As you become older, your metabolism can change and foods that never affected you may now cause nightmares. It is important to know how your system works and to avoid foods that may cause a problem during the night.

Bathroom

Dreaming of being in a bathroom might simply mean that your bladder is full. It could also symbolize a place of privacy. If the bathroom is crowded, the nightmare might indicate you feel as if you lack privacy in your life. If you find yourself in a bathroom meant for the opposite sex, it might suggest that you are crossing boundaries. A bathroom dream can also relate to the elimination of something in your life.

Bear

Dreaming of a bear might speak of your mood (if you've been bearish). The bear traditionally symbolizes forbearance, protectiveness, fearlessness, and possibly the need to rest up in preparation for a draining situation.

Beating

Being beaten in a dream suggests you are releasing the emotion of fear. You fear something in your life is going to hurt you emotionally or hurt your opportunities. Think about the people connected with the situation in your life and whether or not you feel they would hurt you to get ahead. You may also feel "beaten down" about something that has heartfelt meaning to you. Your dream is expressing the depths of your discouragement so you can find your power in the situation. If you are beating someone else in the dream, you have unexpressed anger or frustration about a particular person or situation. Or, you dislike the qualities in yourself that the person in the dream represents.

Bee

A bee's sting is sharp and often sneaks up on you when you least expect it. Therefore, a nightmare about bees might indicate a feeling of being hurt, or a fear that you might get hurt. These creatures are also hard workers that fly from flower to flower gathering pollen to make honey. In this context, they can be a symbol of industriousness, productivity, and success.

Beetle

As with most insects, which are generally considered bothersome, nasty, or dirty creatures, beetles represent unpleasant things in dreams for the most part. However, because the scarab beetle was venerated in ancient Egypt and considered a source of protection, beetles can also signify this element in dreams.

Beggar

Figuratively speaking, dreaming of a beggar indicates a lack, a feeling of falling short or not succeeding, or a sense of being in need. In a more literal sense, however, a beggar is a symbol of those less fortunate and might be an indication of a concern for the poor or a need to be of help. Also, if you are the beggar in your dream, it might be an indication that you will be receiving help when you need it.

Beheading

If you dream about a beheading, notice who the victim is. If it's you, think about where in your life or your relationships you are "losing" your head and not thinking clearly. If another person is being beheaded, you are trying to get rid of some qualities you associate with the other person that you see in yourself as well. Beheading dreams can also be past-life dreams.

Bells

A message of protection or warning, bells might also advise you to center and focus. Alternately, a nightmare with bells tolling might mean a distant friend will die. If you dream of a joyous bell ringing, however, expect success in all aspects of your life.

Bier

If you dream of a bier—the stand used for flowers placed on a coffin—no matter how fresh and beautiful the flowers are, you will know losses.

Big

Often in nightmares you see things bigger than they are in normal, waking life. When something or someone is big in a dream, it indicates that this person or situation looms large in your thoughts, emotions, or actions. If you are bigger in your dreams than in your waking life, you may be growing as a person. Your dream is using the symbol of size to acknowledge that development.

Bleeding

Blood is vital to life, and to dream of bleeding suggests a loss of power and a change for the worse. Blood is also an indication of a wound or injury. Although this might appear in a dream as a literal wound, it might signify some sort of emotional wound or mental scar you are carrying in your waking life.

Blindfold

If you are blindfolded in a bad dream, it indicates that some-one is trying to deceive you or prevent you from seeing something clearly. Conversely, if you are the one doing the blindfolding, consider whether you are trying to pull the wool over someone else's eyes.

Blindness

Blindness in a dream suggests the inability or unwilling-ness to face something in life or to see a person, situation, or some other circumstance for what it really is.

Bomb

A nightmare about a bomb typically represents some sort of volatile situation that is in danger of blowing up. Pay atten-tion to what is going on in this dream. If, for example, you are handling a bomb with care or trying to defuse it, this implies a potentially difficult situation that needs to be dealt with gently or cautiously.

Bones

Bones in a nightmare signify the bottom line—bones are the raw material of a dream. Are the bones scattered? Maybe you're torn in waking life over a decision you have to make. Notice the condition of the bones. That's how you feel about a current nagging issue.

Book

Books represent knowledge, information, and understanding. Pay attention to the age of the book. If it is an old book, for example, the knowledge might come in the form of wisdom from those who have more life experience than you. If the book is pristine and unused, this could be a symbol of new knowledge soon to come your way.

Brain

The brain is the center of mental processes and intelligence, and a dream of this organ is telling you something about your own ways of thinking, or perhaps the thinking of others. Depending on the circumstances, this sort of dream could indicate that you need to give things more thought or consideration or, on the other hand, that things might be weighing too heavily on your mind and you're overly concerned.

Breakdown

To dream of having a mental breakdown indicates you feel completely overwhelmed and out of control in waking life.

Talk to someone and ask for help with the responsibilities on your plate. If you dream your car breaks down on the road, you don't feel ready for a transition occurring in your life, or you worry that you don't have everything in place that you need to be successful.

Break-in

Dreaming of someone breaking into your house means you fear people changing your ideals or getting involved where they shouldn't in your waking life. If you hear noises, it could also be a literal dream and you should investigate. Is the security for your home adequate?

Bridge

Because a bridge connects you from one place to another, in a dream it might represent a crossing from one state of mind to another. Consider the other elements in the dream. Are you crossing dangerous waters? What's waiting for you at the other side of the bridge? What's behind you?

Bull

In dreams, bulls signify masculine energy, stubbornness, creativity, leadership skills, the ego/self (especially for men). They can also mean moving forward too quickly and doing damage in the process. If you dream of a bull, consider the circumstances. If, for example, a bull is killed by a matador (who happens to look like you), a possible interpretation might be that you are getting your bull-headed nature (and temper) under firm control.

Buzzard

If you have a nightmare with a buzzard in it, watch out. An old scandal is likely to surface and injure your reputation. If in your dream a buzzard is sitting on a railroad, you might experience an accident or loss in the near future. Should the buzzard in your dream fly away, all your troubles will be resolved!

C

Cage

A cage represents possession or control, and what you see in the cage is the key to interpreting this sign. A cage full of birds could signify great wealth and many children, whereas a single bird may represent a successful marriage or mate. An empty cage might mean the loss of a family member, whereas a cage full of wild animals might signify that you have control over a particular aspect of your life and that you will triumph over misfortune.

Canal

Canals suggest a journey through the unconscious. Pay attention to other details in the dream. Is the water muddy or clear? Are you traveling alone, or with friends or family?

Cancer

Dreaming of cancer doesn't mean you have it or are going to get it. To be successfully treated for cancer in a dream signals a change for the better. Dreaming of cancer may also symbolize a desperate or foreboding situation, or a draining of resources.

Candles

Usually something of a spiritual nature is suggested by the appearance of candles in dreams. A candle provides light in the dark, or guidance through dark matters or through the unknown and, hence, represents enlightenment in the midst of a bad dream. The flame of a candle can also signify the light that shines within each soul.

The contextual meaning of a candle can be interpreted through its behavior in your dream. If a candle burns down to nothingness, it might indicate a fear or concern about death or impotence. A candle being extinguished could indicate a feeling of being overworked. A steadily burning candle might signify a steadfast character and constancy in friends and family.

Cannibalism

To dream of cannibalism shows that your unconscious feels a need to consume someone else's energy. Are you emotionally draining the people around you? If you dream of someone eating you, be careful of the people with whom you surround yourself. They're not good for your self-esteem.

Castration

Dreaming of castration refers to feelings of inadequacy or impotence in life. You fear the unknown. Think about situations in your life where you feel powerless, helpless, or at the mercy of outside forces.

Cat

Cats can have both positive and negative attributes, depending on your association with them and the surrounding circumstances in the dream. Cats can mean prosperity, playfulness, or quick and agile recuperation. They can also represent independence, the feminine, or sexual prowess. Kittens can mean new ideas, and if you dream of a kitten in a basement it might signify ideas arising from the unconscious mind. Additionally, because cats see well in the dark, they can signify an ability to find illumination in an obscured situation. Cats do have a dark side, too. In a nightmare they might symbolize evil or bad luck, or a catty or cunning person.

Cauldron

Because a cauldron has three legs, witches associate it with the threefold Goddess and her influence. With this in mind, in dreams a cauldron also represents qualities such as fertility and rebirth, and other attributes, including wisdom, rejuvenation, nurturing, creativity, and insight. Though it may appear frightening in your bad dream, a cauldron might actual portend good things.

Cave

Caves are dark, hidden areas, and often represent an obstacle in nightmares. If you can find your way out of one in your dream, this indicates that you'll be able to solve the problem at hand or overcome your obstacle. If, on the other hand, you are lost in a cave, it suggests you still have a way to go when it comes to working out the situation.

Cellar

A cellar often symbolizes the unconscious mind, a place where knowledge is stored or hidden. It can also indicate that the dream comes from the deepest levels of your unconscious, so pay special attention to the way the cellar is lit and to colors and textures. If you dream you are in a cold, damp cellar, it denotes you will soon be oppressed by doubts.

Chain

Seeing a chain in a dream means you are in the process of connecting different experiences, thoughts, or emotions together to make a whole. If you are chained up in the dream, you feel restricted or trapped in some area of your life. If you dream you are chained to other people, you feel your own ability to do what you want is tied to the fortunes or actions of others, whether you like it or not. You need to find your own power to chart your course.

Chase

If you dream of being chased, it is usually an indication that your life (at least according to your unconscious) is not up to par and it's coming back around to get you. In most cases, it doesn't matter who is after you, whether it's your mother-in-law or big, hairy orange monsters. Study the characters in your dreams for clues to help you determine what it is you are running away from in real life.

Chasm

Similar to other dream images of a void, this notion relates back to the fear of falling into something dangerously unknown or empty. This dream can represent obstacles, uncertainty, and also fear of failure, of your capability, or whatever else is concerning you. (See also *Abyss, Cliff, Pit,* and *Precipice.*)

Circling

Circling around and around can mean that you feel you're going in circles without getting anywhere. Pick and choose your battles. Analyze your goals.

Classroom

Are you having the typical nightmare of showing up to class naked, or coming to school unprepared for a test? Often, a classroom dream relates to a personal growth period you are going through. If you dream of finding yourself in a classroom, examine your surroundings and your reason for being there. Is there a positive feeling about the learning environment? Do you recognize who is teaching the class and the subject matter? If you are a teacher having a classroom dream, pay particular attention to what is going on in your everyday classroom life, because the meaning of this dream might be more practical than symbolic.

Cliff

This dream symbol is similar to others related to falling over the edge into something unknown or empty. It can represent obstacles, uncertainty, and also fear of failure, of your capability, and anything else you are unsure about.

Clock

Who isn't acutely aware of the way time seems to fly by? Given that modern life is so tied to "watching the clock," as we constantly attempt to adhere to our monthly, daily, and even hourly schedules, it's no surprise that a dream of a clock symbolizes the passage of time. Pay attention to the details and context clues in a dream of this sort, because the broad scope of time can apply to anything from growing older to an internal clock you might not be realizing you've set for yourself. Do you have certain expectations about when and how soon you would like to accomplish certain things? Could your dream be a subtle reminder to pick up the pace in certain areas, or slow down in others?

Closet

Closets are places where things are stored or hidden. If you are hiding something in your life, your dream might indicate that it is time to release or reveal whatever it is.

Clouds

Dark, stormy clouds rolling in at a low altitude accompanied by flashing lightning might represent your anger regarding a situation. A slate-gray clouded sky might indicate that your views are clouded on a subject. Think about what in your life needs clarity. Dreaming of white, billowing clouds floating in a blue sky suggests that matters are clearing up.

Clown

If you find clowns unnerving, clowns in a nightmare can represent fear of the unknown and the dark, insecure side you feel within. If your reaction toward the clown is one of happiness and joy, having a bad dream about clown might indicate that you are longing for happier, simpler times.

Cockroach

Dreaming of a cockroach can be a literal dream—you saw one while you were awake and it filtered into your nightmares. Think about what you associate with cockroaches. Do you believe they are dirty or carry disease? If so, think about recent events—some situation in your waking life may have made you feel unclean in mind or heart. Roaches are incredible survivors, so depending on your association with them, you might be receiving a message about your own resiliency. Perhaps something in your life that you thought was over has reappeared, and you don't welcome it. Were the dream cockroaches in your house? Because a house represents your life, consider what has been going on in your current life that might be "bugging" you.

Contamination

This dream can be a warning about your health. If you feel you're contaminated in the dream, it may be your body senses something is not right. This dream can also refer to obsessive tendencies or worries that someone else's viewpoint is contaminating your own belief system.

Coffin

A coffin might symbolize a feeling of confinement. Coffins also relate to death; in this case, ask yourself what part of your life might be dead or dying.

Corpse

To dream of yourself as a corpse or to experience your death is not necessarily a prediction of your demise. It could signify a major change in your life, such as the ending of a long-held job or a divorce. If you dream of killing yourself, it could mean that you are going through a traumatic personal transformation, leaving your old life behind. (See also *Suicide*.) If you dream of someone you know as a corpse, then the dream is telling you that an aspect of yourself represented by that person has died. Think about the qualities possessed by the person who is the corpse in the dream, and then reflect on whether or not you have failed to nurture those qualities in yourself. Often the message is an alert that a critical aspect of self has died through neglect or unawareness. Once you know what it is, you can take steps to revive that aspect of yourself if it is vital to your personal happiness.

Crab

Dreaming of a crab signifies moodiness or misdirection, as well as situations that seem to lead nowhere. On another level, crabs are creatures that don't move forward in a straight line; rather, they move sideways. Therefore, if you dream of a crab, ask yourself if there is something in your life that you aren't confronting head-on. Are you skirting around the issue?

Crash

At first glance, a crash that occurs in a nightmare might seem alarming, frightening, and full of destructive implications. However, dreaming of this symbol does not necessarily imply something negative. In fact, it might denote an important event or accomplishment. Dream crashes can also represent something startling, noticeable, or worthy of your attention.

Crocodile

In nightmares, a crocodile represents lies or misrepresentation. Take note of who is near the crocodile, and who interacts with it.

Cross or Crucifix

In Christian tradition, the cross is a symbol of suffering and of burdens to be carried. However, despite the grief and pain that is endured, the cross ultimately symbolizes triumph over adversity.

Crossroads

If you have arrived at a crossroads in your nightmare, this indicates the need to make a choice. If you are hesitant to take either path, this suggests indecision in some matter. In that case, this is a clear indication that making a choice and moving forward is better than standing still without progress.

Crowd

Being lost in a crowd can signify a loss of individuality. You may feel the need to stand out from others. This dream can also describe confusion around you, or even boredom. Maybe it's time to break away or travel.

Crutches

If you have a bad dream about crutches, you may feel you're relying too heavily on something or someone. It can also signify fear of being more independent and venturing out on your own.

Crying

To dream of crying indicates repressed sadness, usually referring to problems of the heart. It can also signify a release from problems. Try not to analyze this dream. Let your unconscious work it out for you. This could be a "release dream" as mentioned in Part 1.

Crystal ball

If you dream of someone seeing your fortune in a crystal ball, that indicates you are contemplating some complicated events in your life. Use caution. Sometimes, a bad dream featuring a crystal ball indicates that the dreamer is trying to make an important decision, and is finding it difficult.

Cursing

If you have a nightmare in which someone is shouting curses at you, it could mean you are upset with yourself for something you've thought or done and feel a need to be punished. If you are the one cursing at others, you are releasing built-up frustration and irritation through the dream.

Cyclops

Beware of dreaming of one eye—it portends that watchful enemies will ferret out a chance to do you harm in your business. Dreaming of a one-eyed man indicates loss and trouble with others plotting against you and your business.

D

Dagger

If you have a nightmare featuring a dagger, you may be feeling threatened emotionally by a situation in your life. If you see daggers in someone's eyes, you feel disapproval from him. If you are the one shooting daggers, you disapprove of something in yourself or in another person but are not directly communicating or trying to clear up the situation.

Darkness

Darkness is a symbol of the unconscious, the hidden, and the unknown. Darkness can also stand for evil, death, and fear. To dream of being overtaken by darkness suggests fear or trepidation over a matter at hand. To dream that you lose a friend or child in the darkness symbolizes that you may be provoked from many different sources.

Darkness represents a lack of illumination, and this can apply in the figurative sense to some aspect of your life. It can signify anything from a situation you're depressed about, to a transition stage as you're becoming accustomed to something new—somewhat akin to "feeling your way around in the dark." A dream of darkness can also relate to a feeling of not being in touch with something, as in being "in the dark" about it.

Dead

The appearance of the dead in a dream typically signifies a warning of some kind. To see the dead living and happy represents a bad influence that may be affecting your life.

Death

Death is the ultimate metamorphosis, the passage from one state of being to another. In the tarot, the Death card means transformation, a major change that hurls you from one way of life to another. In a dream, death is usually a symbol for the same thing.

Only rarely do death dreams portend actual physical death. Many times, dreams about death are simply metaphors for major changes happening in life. These sorts of dreams might be symbolic of your relationships, work, or aspects of personality When you have such a dream, you need to consider whether an area of your life is undergoing transformation. Are you in the middle of a divorce? About to have a baby? Are you about to get married? Are you considering a career change? In this sense, death dreams are not so much about death—they're more about the rebirth that comes from moving from an old stage of life to another stage, as you progress to a new level.

A death or near-death dream involving a living family member or relative, like most death dreams, might be pointing to a major upheaval in that person's life. In that case, the dream acts as a conduit for information.

When dreaming of a friend or relative who has already died, don't worry. This isn't an omen that you or anyone else you know is going to die. It might simply mean that there are parts of this person's personality that have bearing on your own life. If you dream of your grandfather who has already passed on, for example, and the first thing that comes to mind when you think of him is what a hard worker he was, perhaps this is a subtle message that you need to buckle down more in your own endeavors.

Occasionally, a death dream might indicate a death, but not necessarily the death of a person. If there's no sense of fear in the death, the dream can mean you're letting go of something or moving on. On the other hand, a corpse can indicate a lifeless routine. (See also *Dead* and *Dying*.)

Transitional Symbols

As described in the "Death" entry, death is not a literal symbol, but rather a more abstract representation of a difficult transition or upheaval taking place in life. Some other dream symbols that also convey a similar feeling include war, graves, stench, rats, and leeches.

Decapitation

A nightmare about decapitation can happen when you feel a sense of disconnect from your body. You may want to stop certain thought patterns, or wish to reconcile certain ways of thinking with your physical day-to-day life. You may also fear "losing your head" over a situation in your waking life.

Decay

Decay, in a dream, can indicate you are ready to get rid of the old to make room for the new. It can also signify you're neglecting your body or mind. Notice what is decaying in your dream.

Desert

A desert is usually thought of as a desolate place where little grows. It can be symbolic of a fear of death, or of being barren. But a desert can also symbolize hidden beauty and hidden life that is camouflaged to ordinary perceptions. Think about the circumstances of your dream in order to analyze what this desert means to you.

Devil

The quintessential symbol of evil and temptation, if the devil appears in your dreams in his stereotypical form with the usual trappings, it could mean you're hiding something wrong that you've done and your guilty conscience is bothering you. If you are fighting the devil off, he might represent people who are trying to hurt you. The devil may also symbolize a person in your life for whom you have repressed resentment, perhaps a partner or family member.

Digging

What are you digging for? If it's something lost, you might be attempting to retrieve a part of your past. If you are burying something, it indicates a wish to cover up an act, hide your feelings, or hide the facts of a matter.

Dirt

When you dream about earth or dirt, you may feel "dirty" about some recent action. Or, you may be trying to bury feelings that are making you uncomfortable. If you have been stressed at work or in your life in general, you may be dreaming about the ground to symbolize your desire to "ground" yourself and your anxious feelings.

Disappearance

This is a common nightmare in which you are searching for a missing person or item. If it's an object, you're merely coping with a trivial loss. If it's a person who is nowhere to be found, it means you long for a connection with this person. Perhaps you've had a disagreement and you want to make up, but your unconscious knows this may be impossible.

Disinheritance

Not surprisingly, dreaming of disinheritance denotes loss and rough times.

Dismemberment

Dismemberment, in a bad dream, refers to breaking apart before putting things back together. It suggests joining the pieces of your own life puzzle.

Divination tools

If you see or handle these in a nightmare, it likely means that you should be investigating some aspect of your life more closely. These tools represent the need to examine something closely or to gather more information. These tools may also be an indication that you are having a prophesy dream, though that is not necessarily the case in all dreams containing divination tools.

Dog

If in your dream the dog bites, it might indicate a feeling of disloyalty—you're being attacked by man's best friend. To hear dogs barking suggests a message or a warning from your unconscious.

Dragon

Dragons refer to intuition and psychic ability. You may know that something is about to happen, but you don't want to admit it. Dragons also represent authority and power. How do you feel about the dragon in your bad dream?

Drought

Generally an unfavorable omen in a nightmare, droughts represent the absence of life or the drying up of your emotions. Are you with someone in the bad dream? Maybe an unresolved issue between you and someone you are close to is leading to a quarrel or separation.

Drowning

Drowning in a nightmare signifies a deep-rooted fear of delving into your unconscious mind or your deep emotions. You are emotionally overwhelmed at this time in your life, or fear that if you give in to your emotions they will overwhelm you. The more you express and process your emotions, the less overwhelming they will seem.

Drugs

Many times, dreams about drugs are literal—you're under their influence. But being offered drugs in a dream usually refers to negative influences around you. Who is the person offering you the drugs? Drugs can also indicate that a part of you wants to be released from responsibility.

Dusk

Dusk denotes the end of the day. In a dream it can mean the end of happiness or clarity about an issue, or a dark outlook on a matter at hand.

Dying

Dreams of dying represent the ending of an emotional state or situation at hand. To dream that you are going to die suggests an inattention to a particular aspect of your life. To see animals in the throes of death symbolizes bad influences are a threat.

Dynamite

If you dream of dynamite, you fear a potentially explosive situation. Are your repressed emotions about to explode? Examine other features in the nightmare to determine where the problem lies.

E

Earthquake

Dreaming of an earthquake might suggest that personal, financial, or business matters are unstable. Is something upsetting taking place in your life? Earthquakes can also have sexual connotations, such as the desire for sexual release. If other people are in the nightmare, does one of them make the "earth move" for you?

Echo

To hear an echo in your bad dreams can mean you feel nobody is really listening to you or hearing what you're trying to say. Or, it could suggest that your feelings of loneliness are calling to you, encouraging you to connect more with others.

Eclipse

An eclipse suggests a disruption of the normal. When something is "eclipsed," it signifies that a period of activity has ended. An eclipse also speaks of being in a sort of limbo, often between two different phases of life. Also, an eclipse can mean that cosmic forces might be at work in your life. For instance, a lunar eclipse is a warning that you might be trying to run from magical arts or abilities. Conversely, a solar eclipse speaks of someone who doesn't put the proper foundations behind her beliefs and tries to hide from the light of reason.

Eel

An eel, like a snake, can be a symbol of transformation, sexuality, healing, or hidden emotions. Take your cues from what the eel is doing in your dream.

Electrocuted

A nightmare in which you, or someone you see, is being electrocuted signifies you may be shocked by the happenings around you. It also suggests you fear losing power in a close relationship or in your career.

Elevator

What an elevator symbolizes in a bad dream depends on its context. Is it ascending or descending? How fasting is it going? Are you frightened? Exhilarated? A descent in an elevator might indicate a lowering in status or position, or a journey into the unconscious. A stuck elevator might suggest some aspect of your life is presently being delayed. A plunging elevator could indicate a rapid descent into the unconscious, and your fear of losing control in life.

Embarrassment

If you dream of being embarrassed, it indicates you're unsure of what to do next. It also signifies a general lack of overall confidence. Issues from the past that used to bother you have probably resurfaced in your life. Resolve them, and you'll stop having this type of dream.

Empty

An empty room, cup, container, or object is a metaphor for the way you feel about yourself currently. You'd like to fill the object, simply because you're ready for things to go your way. This nightmare symbol also refers to boredom and loneliness.

Enemy

Dreaming of an enemy you know in your waking life signifies that you long for peace with this person but believe it is not possible. An enemy you do not know in waking life usually refers to yourself—you are the enemy. Are you running from the enemy in your nightmare or facing him?

Epaulets

For a man to dream of epaulets means he might be in disfavor among his friends for a time. If a woman dreams of meeting a man wearing epaulets, beware: It denotes she is about to form an unwise alliance that might end in scandal.

Eruption

An eruption, in a dream, means you're holding back in your waking life. You need to release some angst and start things fresh. If the eruption occurs as a volcano, it can refer to repressed sexual desire.

Evening

A nightmare that takes place in the evening suggests uncertain or unrealized hopes. To dream of stars shining suggests present troubles followed by brighter times. A dream of lovers walking in the evening symbolizes separation, the "twilight" of the relationship.

Examination

Ann Faraday, in *The Dream Game*, notes that most of these dreams occur when we feel we're being "tested" or "examined" by someone, as during a job interview, for example, or perhaps in some area of our spiritual lives.

If you have a bad dream in which you are taking an exam, it might indicate a concern about failure, or being unprepared for something. All of us feel unprepared at one time or another, and the examination dream is often a reflection of the uneasy sensation of not being ready for something coming into our lives. Pay attention to the specific elements of this sort of dream, as they will tell you more about the scenario. For example, a stack of tests could suggest you feel you are being tested too often.

When interpreting this dream as it pertains to your own circumstances, make note of whether you're under a dead-line or extreme pressure in your waking life. If you're not, then ask whether there is something in your life that you feel unprepared to cope with.

Excrement

Although excrement in a bad dream may seem embarrass-ing and horrifying, dreaming of excrement can be a good omen. First of all, it can nourish new ideas and beginnings. It also signifies ridding yourself of what you no longer need in order to start anew. In rare cases, it can refer to feelings of being dirty.

Execution

If you're about to be executed or about to witness an execu-tion in your nightmare, it refers to the current sadness and heaviness of heart you feel. If you're depressed, seek profes-sional help. In rare cases, execution can also refer to the end of the old, and a new start, in terms of a way of life.

Exile

To have a nightmare about being in exile usually represents one of three things. You could feel you're being left out or punished by a social circle or relationship you long for. Or, it can mean you feel judged or criticized. Another possibility is that you just feel alone right now.

Explosion

A dream of an explosion could be an attempt by your unconscious to get your attention to a matter of concern. An explosion could suggest a release or an outburst of repressed anger, or an upheaval in your life.

Eye(s)

Eyes have been called the windows of the soul. If you dream of your own eyes, you may be opening up to a new way of seeing things in your waking life or to a heightened sense of your own intuition and inner wisdom. If you get something in your eye or your eye is bloodshot or otherwise unclear, something is obscuring your ability to see a situation clearly. If you are looking deeply into another's eyes in a bad dream, it indicates that you wish you were seen and known for who you really are.

F

Falling

Falling is a common dream symbol and usually an expression of a concern about failure. Nightmares that involve falling can represent a variety of metaphors, including the fallen woman, a fall from grace, or the fall season. This dream can also be a metaphor for falling down on the job, or some other role of responsibility in your life. The interpretation depends, to a large extent, on what is going on in your life at the time or what happened to you within the twenty-four hours preceding the dream. Ask yourself how you feel as you're falling: Do you feel terrified? Helpless? Out of control? Or is the sensation pleasant? If so, how?

In most falling dreams, the dreamer never lands. If you do hit the ground, it could mean that you've struck bottom in a matter.

Fat

A bad dream in which you are fat might relate to a concern about your diet or your appearance, but it could also be a metaphor for wealth and abundance, or overindulging.

Fence

A dream of a fence can indicate that you feel "fenced in." A fence can block you or it can protect you. If you are "on the fence," the dream might suggest that you are undecided about something.

Fever

To dream you are suffering from a fever suggests a needless worry over a small affair. Be patient, and it will work itself out. This unhappy dream may also be a response from your body letting you know you are getting sick and that you actually have a temperature.

Fight

To fight in a dream might represent a conflict or the need to resolve an issue. Pay attention to other details in the dream in order to interpret it. Are you winning or losing a fight? Are you fighting with a loved one, someone else you know, or a perfect stranger?

Fire

Fire represents the power of light over darkness, and it is generally a favorable symbol to the dreamer. It often represents continued prosperity and fortune—so long as the dreamer is not burned. If you're on fire in your dream, it's probably a metaphor for passion; it's as if you are burning with desire. Fire can also symbolize a variety of other things, including wrath, destruction, purification, cleansing, illumination, and a spiritual awakening. Look at other metaphors. For instance, fire might indicate a heated situation. What are you getting "fired up" about? Are you (or another figure in the dream) concerned about "being fired" or "getting burned"? Additionally, a dream of fire might indicate a call to gather with a community, as people traditionally have gathered around fires for meals, storytelling, or rituals.

Flames

To see flames in a bad dream represents the need for purity and purification of thoughts and deeds. Take note of what is on fire to determine the exact meaning. Flames can also refer to hidden passion or a crush you prefer not to admit to.

Flogging

To be flogged in a nightmare signifies you feel you should be punished for something you've done or for treating someone badly. To see someone flogged in a dream indicates the need to settle some emotional issues in your life.

Flood

Dreaming of a flood might suggest that you feel overwhelmed by a rising awareness of the unconscious aspects of your being. A dream of flooding can also serve as a warning that personal matters are spilling over into other areas of your life. Alternately, a flood can relate to a release of sexual desires or a need to do so.

Fly (the insect, not the action)

You may be experiencing some pesky setbacks that are causing disappointment now. Try to be patient. It may take a little longer, but things should go as planned. If you have a nightmare in which you are being bitten by a fly, you are being annoyed by someone in your circle of acquaintances.

Fog

Dreaming of foggy conditions indicates a lack of clarity in some aspect of your life. Fog can also symbolize something hidden or something you're not seeing. Keep in mind that fog is usually short-lived and when it lifts, you will gain a new sense of clarity.

Forest

A forest suggests an exploration of the unconscious. It also can symbolize a need or desire to retreat from everyday life, to restore and revitalize your energies. Finding yourself in a dense forest during a nightmare can signify unpleasantness at home. A forest fire in a dream has a few meanings. In a good dream it might symbolize the successful completion of your plans, with wealth and prosperity to follow, since regrowth is such an essential aspect of a forest fire's aftermath. However, if you are trapped in a burning forest, or if you are trying to escape the fire, you may be trying to come to terms with a real-life difficulty.

Forked line/Fork in the road

You'll have to make a decision soon. This symbol in an unsettling dream indicates that you should choose the simplest route for now.

Fortune-teller/Fortune-telling

You are looking for answers of a mystical nature. A nightmare involving a fortune-teller may mean that you have anxiety about the future and want to be reassured. What are you concerned about? Seek the help of people you trust in your waking life for advice and reassurance.

Fraud

Dreaming of fraud can be a warning about yourself or others. Who is committing fraud in the nightmare? If you're the one committing fraud, it's possible you've shown a side of yourself to someone and now feel vulnerable.

Frost

Frost, like ice, may represent an emotional state of the dreamer or another person in the bad dream. To see a friend or lover in frost could mean chilly feelings regarding the relationship.

Frostbite

If you dream of frostbite, it could indicate that a part of you feels stuck in a current situation or relationship. It could also mean you're not expressing yourself as well as you could or should.

Funeral

Rather than death, this usually refers to saying goodbye to a way of thinking or a way of life. It indicates change and transformation. In rare cases, it can refer to worry about growing older. Pay attention to your emotions during the funeral nightmare—that will indicate which meaning the symbol represents.

Fungus

Fungus in your bad dream can refer to an actual physical problem. It can also symbolize a situation in your life that's growing out of control.

Fury

To be in a fury in your nightmare indicates a certain anger you feel toward yourself with regard to recent decisions you've made. If you feel fury toward another person in your dream, you may harbor resentment toward her. You'll need to deal with this soon.

Fuse

If a fuse blows in your dream, this refers to repressed anger you have toward someone. It can also signify unexpected, startling news to come.

G

Gang

If you encounter a gang in your bad dream, it means you're feeling nervous about a situation you're currently in, and the need to escape is great. You may also feel that others have "ganged up" on you and you are trying to hold your own in the situation. Confront the problem, and you'll cease having this unnerving dream.

Garbage

A nightmare that features garbage suggests a need to get rid of old, worn-out ideas, or excess baggage in your life. Ask yourself if you are clinging to something or some condition that you no longer need.

Gate

A gate might represent a portal from one state of being to another. Is there a gatekeeper? Do you meet the gatekeeper's criteria for passage to the next level?

Ghost

An apparition or ghost appearing in a dream might suggest that something in your life is elusive or out of reach. If a person who has died appears in a dream, consider your past relationship to that person and what that individual symbolized in your life. A ghost of a living relative or friend in a dream might symbolize that you are in danger from someone you know. If that ghost appears haggard it might signify an early death or the end of a friendship.

Giant

If you find yourself faced with a terrifying giant in a nightmare, you're aware of problems looming over you that you're afraid or unwilling to face. If the giant is not the antagonist in the dream, it could indicate that your life is about to expand in a big way.

Gloom

If the scene around you in your bad dream is gloomy, you probably feel this way about your current state of affairs. What's depressing you? Look to the other figures in the dream and examine whether or not they're positive influences in your waking life.

Grave

Like many symbols in nightmares, a grave is one that grabs and draws your attention—especially if it's your grave. A grave can portend a death, but not necessarily a physical one. It might mean that you're leaving the old behind, moving on to something new, as in experiencing a transition. As a metaphor, a grave also suggests that you might be dealing with a grave matter.

Grief

Grief, in a bad dream, can be a good thing because it helps you deal with a problem you're facing in waking life. Normally, you are actually suffering from something harsh in both the dream and in real life. The dream is helping you process the emotion. This could be one of the "release dreams" discussed in Part 1.

Grotesque

A nightmare that features something grotesque refers to a fear you have within yourself. What is grotesque in the nightmare? What does it signify for you? If a part of yourself is misshapen or grotesque, you feel a quality you possess is negative or unhealthy and becoming visible to others.

Gun

A gun in your possession can symbolize protection, but it is also a phallic symbol and a sign of aggressive male behavior. If you shoot yourself, the act is what's important, not the gun. (See *Suicide.*)

Gypsy

The typical notion of gypsies is that they never stay rooted in one place, and in dreams, they might imply wandering, restlessness, and movement. If you encounter a gypsy in your dreams, it might also be an indication of unexpressed psychic potential.

H

Hail

To dream of being in a hailstorm, or to hear hail hitting against the house, represents being besieged by a troubling matter, thoughts, or emotions. However, if you dream of watching hail fall through sunshine and rain, it might suggest that fortune and pleasure will shine on you after a brief period of trouble or misery.

Hammer

A hammer might suggest strength or power. However, because it can be used for either constructive or destructive purposes, how the hammer is used is the key to its meaning.

Hand

A nightmare about a hand (or hands) is open to numerous interpretations, depending on what the hand (or hands) is doing and the surrounding circumstances. A hand that is grasping at something might indicate a fear of death. As a metaphor, a hand can suggest that something important is "at hand." Ugly and malformed hands point to disappointment and poverty. A detached hand represents solitude; people might fail to understand your views and feelings in a matter. Burning your hands in a dream suggests that you have overreached your abilities and will suffer some loss because of it.

Hang

If you see someone being hanged in your dream, you are afraid of being judged without having the chance to explain yourself. If you dream you're being hanged for something you've done, it means you have enormous guilt. This is a warning to stop being overcritical of yourself.

Harming others

If in a bad dream you harm others, through deceit, telling lies, or injuring their reputations in some way, it indicates that your own reputation is about to plummet.

Havoc

If you dream of havoc or bedlam around you, you're feeling overwhelmed in your life right now. If you're the one causing the havoc in your nightmare, it means you are aware that others deem your behavior less than satisfactory.

Hearing voices

Dreaming that you are hearing pleasant voices indicates joyous reconciliations will happen in your future. If the voices are angry, expect disappointments; if the voices are weeping, expect to have a sudden outburst of anger. If you hear the voice of God, honorable people will soon praise you for your unselfishness and generosity.

Hearse

If you dream of seeing a hearse, it may indicate you sense some problems ahead that you feel could be deadly. If you dream of riding in a hearse, it signifies that you're saying goodbye to a certain part of yourself. Be ready for new things to come.

Heart

To see a heart might relate to romantic inclinations. Is there a "heart throb" in your life? Alternately, the image might suggest you get to the "heart of the matter." On the negative side, if your heart is bleeding, it could mean that excessive sympathy is becoming a burden for you or the recipient, or both.

Heights

To dream of being afraid of heights signifies that you're not doing enough in your career. You may have a fear of success, and consequently your ambition is being thwarted. If you love heights, then you are soaring to new heights in some aspect of your life, or you are gaining new perspective on a situation or relationship.

Hell

Beware if hell is a central element in a nightmare. If in your dream you are actually in hell with the devil, this indicates that you are in danger of falling into temptations that could destroy you and your reputation. If you dream of friends being trapped in hell, you will soon hear of your friends' misfortunes.

Helmet

Wearing a helmet in a dream denotes protection. The helmet could also symbolize that you need to guard your time, thoughts, or ideas.

Hemorrhage

A nightmare that features hemorrhaging denotes that your life force is being sapped by a situation or person in your life. Someone or something is emotionally draining you and you feel your energy is being depleted.

Hermaphrodite

To dream of a hermaphrodite could mean two things. Either you're trying to unify the different sides of yourself, or you've been presented with two choices and you have an important decision to make.

Hermit

Dreaming of a hermit is a sign that you need to be patient and wait for things to right themselves. Now is not the time to take action. It also means you enjoy the time you spend alone, and that it is time to listen to your inner wisdom.

Hiccup

Most likely, some plans you had or will have in the near future have been thwarted and you're searching to find out why. Hiccupping, in a nightmare, also refers to making too much out of trivial matters.

Hiding

If you're hiding in a bad dream, it signifies that you're embarrassed or may feel guilty about some of your recent behavior. It could also point to a desire to get away from the rigors of daily life.

Hitchhiking

To dream of hitchhiking is a message that you've been too dependent on others. You've relied on them to get you where you want to go, and now you need to take more responsibility for your actions. It may also be a warning that you've put yourself in danger in some situation and that you should be more careful in the near future.

Hitting

If you are hit in a bad dream, it means you feel others are taking advantage of you and are judging you harshly. On the other hand, if you dream of hitting someone or something, you may have resentment or anger bottled up and you need to express it.

Hole

Seeing a hole in a nightmare can symbolize a fear of the unknown. It may also refer to sexual desire and the need for sex in order to feel complete. A hole in your clothing indicates financial concerns.

Homesickness

Being homesick in a dream is usually quite literal—you long for the way things were in the past. It can also portend a call or visit from someone you once knew and haven't heard from in a while.

Hospital

Finding yourself in a hospital suggests a need for healing, or a concern about your health. Seeing someone else in a hospital might indicate that person is in a weakened condition. If you work in a hospital, the meaning of the bad dream could relate to work matters. In the latter case, other circumstances in the dream should be examined.

Hurricane

Destructive and unpredictable, hurricanes can suggest different meanings depending on their context in the dream. To hear and/or see a hurricane coming at you symbolizes a feeling of torture and suspense regarding a matter in which you are trying to avert failure. To dream of looking at the debris of a hurricane suggests you will come close to calamity, but will be saved by the efforts of others. A nightmare in which you are in a house that is shattered by a hurricane and you are trying to save someone caught in the rubble might mean your life will suffer many changes but that there is still no peace in domestic or business matters. To see people dead and wounded suggests that you are concerned over the troubles of others.

I

Ice

Ice can symbolize an emotional state of the dreamer or a person in the dream. Are you receiving an "icy reception"? If you are in a tenuous situation, you could be "skating on thin ice." In a sexual context, ice represents frigidity. If you have a nightmare in which ice is floating in a clear stream, it signifies an interruption of happiness. Dreaming of eating ice portends sickness.

Iceberg

To dream of hitting an iceberg means that things have been rocky emotionally, or you sense they soon will be. It's a good indication that, though there are obstacles to overcome, you'll be all right if you look for the warning signs and process your emotions as they emerge.

Icicles

Icicles represent danger or your concern over a matter that is hanging over you in some way. To dream of icicles falling off trees or the eaves of a house may suggest that some misfortune will soon disappear. To dream of icicles on evergreens symbolizes that a bright future may be overshadowed by doubt.

Idiot

Seeing an idiot in your bad dream signifies your unconscious is aware that you're about to make a very foolish decision. If you dream of being an idiot, it means your self-confidence is low right now and you need to do something to bolster it.

Illiteracy

Dreaming that you can't read or write has two meanings. Either you're having trouble expressing yourself in waking life, or there's a breakdown in communication with someone close to you.

Illness

If you dream of being ill, ask yourself if you need to be cared for and pampered. This nightmare might also be a message to watch your health.

Impotence

A bad dream in which you are impotent means you feel insignificant and powerless in some area of your life. Rarely does this dream actually refer to sexual problems.

Incest

A dream of a sexual encounter with someone within your family is not necessarily a warning about incest. Examine your relationship with the person in question. If you've argued with this person or you're alienated from this family member, the dream might be your inner self expressing your love in a shocking way that will catch your attention.

Indifference

This nightmare is indicative of how you think others view you. If someone is indifferent toward you in a dream, it could mean you worry this is how he really feels. Your unconscious may be letting you know that he does truly feel indifferent toward you. If you are indifferent toward someone or some situation, think about whether or not you wish to continue that relationship or activity. Instead, put your energy toward something that has greater meaning for you.

Infidelity

Many times, dreaming that your partner is being unfaithful is simply a fear you have of being abandoned or cheated on in waking life. However, sometimes this is a warning sign that the deed is actually being done.

Injured

A dream of being injured refers to your current emotional state. Perhaps someone has used harsh words with you lately or has let you down in some way that has affected you deeply.

Insects

In general, insects represent small aggravations or things that are "bugging" you. Specific meanings can change dramatically depending on which type of insect appears as well as the overall context of the dream. For example, if you dream of ants, you might be feeling "antsy" about a particular matter.

Insults

To be insulted in your dream means you are being hard on yourself. What are the insults? Do you feel this way toward yourself? Many times, if you're insulting someone in your dream, this is how you feel toward the person you're insulting.

Interview

Being interviewed in a bad dream is similar to taking an examination. It suggests you're being judged. If you're surprised by the interview, it could indicate that you are feeling unprepared.

Invalid

A nightmare about an invalid might indicate that you (or someone else) feel weak or incapable of living independently.

Itching

If you have an itch in waking life, it could translate into your dream. As a metaphor, itching in a bad dream refers to little nagging problems you need to deal with as soon as possible.

J

Jail

In a nightmare, a jail might indicate that you're feeling restricted or confined and fear being punished. Or you might believe that you should be punished. Dreaming of being a jailer suggests the desire to control others or to gain more control of your own life.

Jaws

Do you feel like you're under attack? Jaws can be the entry point to an archetypal journey into the underworld. Such a bad dream might also relate to a disagreement.

Jealousy

Who are you jealous of in the dream? Is it someone you know or is it a stranger? If it's someone you know, this may be a literal dream. If it's someone you don't know, perhaps you are feeling a strong sense of inadequacy.

Jet

Dreaming of the stone jet warns of sadness ahead.

Judge

If you're the judge, the dream suggests that you have a choice to make. A judge can also represent justice or fairness. Alternately, a judge might stand for a part of you that criticizes your impulsive behavior. Or perhaps you're concerned that you are being judged. If so, think about who it is that's judging you.

Jungle

A jungle might represent a hidden, dark part of the self that you've been avoiding. Your unconscious might be telling you of a need to explore this part of yourself. It could also represent a great, untapped fertility for spiritual growth within you.

Junk

If you dream of junk or clutter, ask yourself if you're clinging to the past, to things or ideas that are no longer useful. If something you value appears as junk in a dream, it may indicate that you need to reassess your values.

K

Key

Keys represent entrance: They open doors, start cars, and allow us to get inside our homes and offices. If you have a bad dream about losing keys, this signifies that you are being denied entrance or access to somewhere or something. If, on the other hand, you recover your keys in a dream, it indicates that you are regaining that access.

A key can also stand for a part of yourself that you've locked away. In that case, the same notions of losing or retrieving a key would apply, just directly to yourself. A dream of this sort might also indicate you hold the key to your own concerns.

Kicked out

To get kicked out of a place denotes sadness about not fitting into a group or social situation. In waking life, this may also mean you push people's buttons or limits too much and too often.

Kicking

Kicking, in a dream, represents hostility and anger. Are you the one kicking or is someone kicking you? Kicking also indicates a desire to get revenge on someone who has wronged you.

Killing

A bad dream of killing someone is probably not a warning that you might turn into a killer. Instead, the meaning is more likely a symbolic act of aggression. Whom did you kill and how is that person involved in your life? If you don't recognize the person, the nightmare might symbolize killing off an unwanted part of yourself.

Kneeling

In basic terms, kneeling is equivalent to not standing up. By association, when you're not standing, you can't walk, advance, or move forward well. Not surprisingly, then, a nightmare in which you're kneeling could have ties to all these things. Consider whether there is something or someone in your life holding you back, or someone or something you can't "stand up to." Kneeling also puts you at a different level than one who is standing, so consider whether or not you feel as if you don't have "equal ground" on something.

On another level, kneeling is a common sign of reverence and prayer. Therefore, it can also relate to feelings of God's power and authority and, by extension, the power and authority of anyone else who is important in your life—a parent, for example. In this case, consider whether you might be blowing that sense of authority out of proportion, if it makes you feel subjugated to the point of kneeling before that person.

Knife

A knife is a symbol of aggression and the male sexual organ. Examine the other aspects of the nightmare. Are you being stabbed in the back? Do you hold the knife or is someone threatening you with it? A rusty knife might symbolize dissatisfaction, a sharp knife worry, and a broken knife defeat.

Knot

Knots tie things together and in dreams they can signify the binding of negative or unwanted energy—or holding energy in place until it's needed. Dreaming of knots also suggests you might be "all tied up" about something—that worries or anxieties are troubling you. You might feel as if you're "tied in a knot." Alternately, if you or someone close to you is "tying the knot," the nightmare might signify a concern about an upcoming marriage.

L

Laboratory

A laboratory is a place where experiments are conducted. The implication is that you are unsatisfied with a present situation and experimenting with something new. You might also be testing a relationship with someone.

Labyrinth

Labyrinths are full of twists and turns, and as such, are a symbol of being lost and confused. A nightmare of a labyrinth or maze might indicate that you feel trapped in a situation or a relationship and are looking for a way out. It might also refer to the intricacies of a spiritual journey.

Lance

A lance, by Freudian standards, is a phallic symbol, one of masculinity and aggression. Who is using the lance in your dream? Do you have intimate or aggressive feelings toward this person in waking life? Do you feel you need to defend yourself in a situation?

Lawsuits

Nightmares of legal matters suggest the dreamer is being judged, or feels judged by someone in the waking world.

Leeches

Leeches are nightmarish creatures that suck blood. If you dream of leeches, ask yourself if some person or situation in your life is draining your energy. Leeches can also symbolize difficult transitions.

Leopard

If you dream of a leopard attacking you, you might encounter many difficulties working toward future success. But if you kill the leopard, you will be victorious in life. Dreaming of a caged leopard means that although your enemies surround you, they will fail to injure you.

Lightning

A nightmare that features a lightning strike indicates a flash of inspiration or sudden awareness about the truth of a matter. Lightning can also mean a purging or purification, or fear of authority or death.

Lion

To dream of a lion signifies that you are driven by a great force. Subduing a lion indicates victory in a matter. If you are overtaken by the lion, the dream suggests you might be vulnerable to an attack of some sort. A caged lion might mean you will succeed as long as the opposition to your goal is held in check. Lions also represent authority, protection, and ferocity when defending something you love.

Lizard

Because lizards shed their skins, it stands to reason that dreaming of one suggests the ability to break away from the old and begin anew.

Loss

Losing something in a dream often means your unconscious is working out the loss of something very real in your waking life. What do you feel you're parting with? Is it a healthy thing or something you actually still need? The thing you lose in the dream is often not literal; it's a symbol for the actual lost object, relationship, or opportunity.

M

Magic

In nightmares, the presence of magic represents personal power that requires responsibility and control. In another sense, magic could point to the magical aspects of creativity or, on the darker side, to deceit and trickery.

Map

A map in a dream suggests you're searching for a new path to follow or are being guided in a new direction.

Mask

Masks hide our appearances and our feelings from others, but the nightmare could also indicate that you are hiding your emotions regarding a particular matter from yourself. If others are wearing masks, perhaps you are confronted with a situation in which you think someone is not being truthful.

Maze

Mazes are full of twists and turns and as such, they often represent a complicated situation that you can't find your way out of.

Missing class

Like dreams of examinations, if in your nightmare you forgot to go to a class, this might suggest that you are worried about being unprepared.

Mist

Like fog, mist indicates a period of temporary uncertainty or lack of clarity. Seeing others in a mist may mean that you will profit by their misfortune and uncertainty.

Moon

If you dream of the moon, and especially if it is the predominant feature in a dream, this could imply the development of your intuitive senses. Once believed to be the source of a witch's power, the phase of the moon influences the meaning of this symbol in your dreams. A full moon, for example, would indicate coming into full awareness of potential, whereas a waning moon might indicate that inner resources are wanting.

The moon is also a source of illumination and might symbolize light reflecting in the dark if you need clarity or direction in a situation or issue in your life.

Signs and Coincidences

Dreams and waking life are not so different. Dreams come from your subconscious, a part of you. Therefore, you can take the signs and coincidences from your dreams and apply them to your life. If you watch for prophecy and heed your guides (spiritual, animal, and otherwise), you can change the way things are going and plan for your future. That's what dream interpretation is all about.

Mother-in-law

A dream in which your mother-in-law appears suggests that you are looking for a deeper connection or to resolve problems with her. Think about the qualities in your mother-in-law that you admire or that trouble you. You will find these same qualities in yourself. Perhaps your nightmare is asking you to become less engaged in someone else's life; allow her to take more responsibility for herself.

Mouse

A nightmare that includes a mouse indicates frugality through innovation.

Mud

Mud represents the need for cleansing or purification in dreams.

Mule

Mules are known for their contrary behavior, as in "stubborn as a mule." To have a bad dream about a mule suggests that you might be acting in a stubborn manner that others find annoying. Mules also are work animals. Consider whether you are rebelling against some aspect of your job or career.

Murder

Murder symbolizes repressed anger, either at yourself or others. If you murder someone you know, consider your relationship with that person. If you're the one murdered, then the dream may symbolize a personal transformation.

N

Nail

A nail in a bad dream can have a variety of meanings, so consider the context. For example, to "nail it down" suggests putting something together or holding it together. Or, if you "hit the nail on the head," you've gotten something exactly right, articulated something perfectly, and so on.

Naked/Nudity

The first reaction to such a dream might be to consider its practical implications. If, for instance, you are about to embark on a trip and have a nightmare in which you are naked while traveling, check your luggage to make sure you're taking everything you need.

But like other common dreams, the nudity is more likely symbolic. Finding yourself naked in a public place, such as on a busy street, is embarrassing. If you've had such a nightmare, you probably were relieved when you realized it was a dream. Being nude in a dream points to a feeling of being exposed or vulnerable. This type of dream could mean you're exposed to the criticism of others, but it might also symbolize a wish for exposure, as in a desire to be seen or heard. Are you looking for exposure, for example, to publicize something you've done? In a case like that, the dream might even suggest that the exposure you've been seeking is about to occur.

A bad dream of being naked can also relate to a need to bare the truth—or hide it. Think about whether or not you are hiding something that you've done from the public view. In either case, a nudity dream brings to light a concern.

Needle

A dream of a needle and thread might indicate that a matter is being sewn up, or a deal is being completed. A needle might also suggest that someone is needling you. A nightmare that involves threading a needle symbolizes that you might be burdened with caring for others; to look for a needle augurs useless worries. To break a needle in a bad dream signifies loneliness and poverty.

Night

A night setting for a nightmare might suggest something is hidden or obscured, and there might be a need to illuminate something in your life. Being surrounded by night in a bad dream suggests oppression and hardship.

Obstacles

Obstacles in dreams always translate metaphorically. In other words, you have placed a burden or problem in front of yourself, and all you need to do is step back and see the picture more clearly in order to solve the dilemma.

Odor

If you smell an odor in your dream, it could be literal. You might smell an odor in waking life and it filters into the dream. Otherwise, good odors signify good luck and bad odors signify the opposite.

Officer

An officer, whether military, police, or corporate, represents an authority figure. Having a nightmare of an officer, especially if you don't know the person, can suggest a fear or wariness of authority figures or a need for guidance from a person with authority.

Old man

If the old man guides or directs you in some way, he is, in Jungian thought, an archetypal figure. If the man appears to be weak or injured in some way, he could symbolize some part of you that needs attention or someone in your life who needs your help. It could also mean that you need to rede-fine your beliefs about aging.

Old woman

In Jungian terms, an old woman is an archetypal symbol of the power of the feminine, or the gatekeeper between life and death. If she is weak or injured, she may represent a part of you that needs attention or someone in your life who needs your help.

Onyx

According to traditional dream symbolism, onyx portends arguments. Take note of who or what is near the onyx in your bad dream.

Operation

To have a nightmare about an operation could mean you're worried about some aspect of your health and you'd like to become more physically fit. It also represents change from a current situation.

Owl

An owl represents both wisdom and mystery and is a symbol of the unconscious. Because owls have excellent night vision, they might also signify illumination in a dark situation. In addition, owls symbolize messages and news; pay attention to your inner voice in reacting to these missives. If, in your nightmare, you hear an owl screech, it means you will be shocked with bad news.

P

Past lovers

Many sexual dreams are a commentary on your past and present relationships, and dreams that feature past lovers are no exception. In outrageous dream circumstances, all your past lovers might even show up at the same party, or in the same bed. This sort of bad dream is an indication that you need to analyze past involvements that continue to impact current relationships. If you have a nightmare of this sort, it's important to look for patterns that mark your relationships. This is especially critical if you've had a series of unsuccessful relationships or affairs that began filled with promise and ended badly.

Pepper

If you dream of pepper burning your tongue, it could mean you feel hurt by sharp words recently spoken—by yourself or someone else. To sneeze from pepper in a bad dream indicates that something in your life is irritating you and you want to get rid of it.

Pill

Taking a pill in a nightmare suggests you feel you might be required to go along with something unpleasant in your waking life.

Pit

The idea of a dark, bottomless pit is related to other dream symbols that represent unknown emptiness. Dreaming of a pit is typically an indication that you are faced with obstacles, fear of failure, or some sort of other uncertainty.

Police

Police officers represent authority; they uphold the law. A bad dream of the police might serve as a warning against breaking the law or bending rules. It might suggest a fear of punishment. Alternately, the dream could indicate a desire for justice and a need to punish the wrongdoers in a matter of concern to you.

Porcupine

A dream that includes a porcupine warns that you should be on guard.

Precipice

Standing on the edge of a precipice represents a fear of falling into emptiness or the unknown. This is a dream of obstacles and uncertainty. (See also *Abyss, Chasm, Cliff*, and *Pit.*)

Prison

Constraint and restriction are implied. If you see yourself at work in a prison, the dream might suggest that you've limited your creativity or that you feel it's difficult to "escape" your job for a better one.

Puppet

A frightening dream about a puppet might indicate that you feel manipulated in some aspect of your life. Alternately, if you are controlling the puppet, pulling the strings, the dream could be warning you that you're acting in a manipulative manner.

Q

Quarrel

A nightmare about a quarrel might indicate that an inner turmoil is plaguing you. If the person you're quarreling with is identifiable, consider the relationship you have with that person and see if you can identify the area of disagreement. The dream may hold clues that indicate a way to resolve the differences.

Quicksand

A bad dream of quicksand indicates that you need to watch where you are headed. If you're already in the quicksand, then you're probably mired in an emotional matter and feel as if you can't escape. It could refer to either business or personal matters.

R

Rapids

Rapids represent danger and a fear of being swept away by emotions.

Rat

Rats are generally associated with filth and dilapidation. Nightmares that feature a rat or rats might suggest the deterioration of a situation. Ask yourself who the "rat" is in your life. Because rats can also be a symbol for difficult changes, go with this theme and consider if you fear that something in your life is deteriorating.

Raven

In dreams, ravens represent some sort of warning. Take note of what else is in your dream when the ravens appear, because that might give you some insight into what you should be wary of.

Road

A road is a means of getting from one place to another. Notice the condition of the road in your nightmare: A smooth and straight road suggests the path ahead is easy. On the other hand, a road with dips and curves could indicate that you need to be aware, flexible, and ready for change. A roadblock suggests detours in your path.

Ruins

To dream of something in ruins suggests the deterioration of some condition in your life. But keep in mind that when things fall apart an opportunity to rebuild inevitably appears.

Running

When you run in a nightmare, it can be either toward or away from something. You might want to escape from something or to reach a safe place. Depending on the circumstances, the dream might indicate either that you need to hurry, or that you're rushing around too much and need to rest.

S

Sacrifice

To see yourself sacrificed in a dream suggests you're giving up something important for the sake of others. Closely examine your feelings about the matter. Decide what changes, if any, need to be made in your life and in your relationships.

School

If you have a nightmare that takes place in a school, what happens in the school is important in the interpretation. If you're late to class or show up to take a test without ever having gone to class, you feel unprepared for something in your life. If you're looking for a school or classroom, the dream could be telling you that expanding your education is in order.

Scissors

This could mean there is something in your life you want to cut off. Dreaming of scissors also might indicate a need to "cut it out." Pay attention to the person holding the scissors in your nightmare—the scissors could be a symbol for someone in your life who is acting "snippy."

Screaming without sound

If you have a nightmare in which you yell, and yet no sound comes out, it's probably associated with an instance in your waking life in which you feel unable to voice your feelings. Do you feel uneasy speaking up to specific people or in particular situations in your life? Consider how you can begin taking steps to "find" your voice and express yourself.

Sea

In a nightmare, the sea represents unfulfilled longings.

Searching

Dreams that involve searching are usually less about the thing you are searching for, although that could provide you with contextual clues, and more about the search itself. Searching in a dream is typically a metaphor for something you are looking for—or something you need—in your waking life. If, for instance, you have a dream in which you are searching for a place to make love, where you search from house to house, place to place, or town to town, the dream is more about the search for a place than about sex itself. Such dreams are metaphors for a search for intimacy.

Sex

According to Sigmund Freud, all dreams are linked with sexual issues. Freud was writing during the Victorian era, when talk of sex was taboo, and his ideas helped free the Western world from the repressive strictures of the era. However, Freud's view that the sex drive powers virtually all our dreams is no longer accepted. In fact, it's now thought by a number of dream researchers that some sex dreams might not have anything at all to do with sex.

Sexual dreams can contain clues to important personal needs, desires, fears, and changes. For instance, people recovering from illness, depression, surgery, or the grieving process, might suddenly and inexplicably begin having sexual dreams. Such dreams appear to be associated with an increase in physical vitality and a greater sense of aliveness, although they might precede physical recovery in some cases. Dreams such as this often come across as almost humorous, given recent physical challenges. Yet, these dreams serve as reminders that although you've been through hell, you're still very much alive.

Shadow

This is another one of Jung's archetypes. Dreaming of your shadow might suggest that you need to address hidden parts of yourself. Perhaps you do not accept these darker aspects of your personality and project them onto others.

The nightmare might also suggest that you need to incorporate the shadow side into your psyche.

Shovel

A tool for digging, a shovel in a bad dream might indicate that you are searching for something or are about to embark on a quest for inner knowledge. A shovel might also represent labor or hard work ahead. A broken shovel could mean you are experiencing frustration in your work.

Sickness/Illness

If you have a nightmare about being ill, ask yourself if you're in need of being cared for and pampered. This dream might also be a message to watch your health. To dream of a family member who is sick represents some misfortune or issue that is troubling your domestic life.

Skull

To dream of a skull and crossbones is a traditional sign of danger and possibly death—a warning.

Smoke

If you dream of smoke filling a room, it suggests that a matter in your life is being obscured. On the other hand, if the smoke is dissipating, clarity is imminent.

Snake

A snake is an archetypal image that can suggest numerous interpretations. In mythology, snakes are symbols of wisdom and fertility. In the ancient Greek and Roman cultures, snakes were also symbols of the healing arts. Like lizards, snakes shed their skins—a symbol of renewal. Therefore, dreaming of a snake could mean that some type of new life or opportunity is going to begin. According to some Eastern traditions, the snake is related to a power that rises from the base of the spine and is a symbol of transformation. For example, the ancient symbol of the snake swallowing its own tail represents the way nature feeds on and renews itself.

However, snakes also often symbolize the dangers of the underworld. In the Bible, the snake represents temptation, forbidden knowledge, and the source of evil. Snakes often appear in fairy tales as tricksters who are wise but wily. The Freudian interpretation relates snakes to the male genitalia, and in dreams snakes are also linked to wisdom or sex, or both. Jung considered the archetypal image of snakes to represent an awareness of the essential energy of life and nature. When trying to interpret a dream about a snake, pay attention to how you view snakes symbolically and consider other aspects of the dream.

Snow

Because snow is a solidified form of water, it can stand for frozen emotions. If the snow is melting, frozen feelings are thawing. To find yourself in a snowstorm may represent uncertainty in an emotional matter or sorrow at failing to enjoy some long-expected pleasure.

Spear

Thrusting a spear at someone in a nightmare may represent an effort to thrust your will on another person. If the spear is hurled over a field or toward a mountain or an ocean, the dream may mean you are making a powerful statement to the world.

Spider

Spiders are industrious and detailed in their web-spinning, and in dreams they can symbolize your approach to your work. A confrontation with a large spider could signify a quick ascent to fame and fortune, unless the large spider bites you, in which it may represent the loss of money or reputation. Getting caught in a spider's web may indicate that you are feeling trapped by a situation in your waking life.

Statue

A bad dream with a statue or statues could signify a lack of movement in your life. Statues are also cold and can symbolize frozen feelings.

Stillborn

To dream of a stillborn infant indicates a premature ending or some distressing circumstance in a matter at hand.

Stones

Stones can represent small irritations or obstacles that must be overcome. Seeing yourself throw a stone in a dream could mean that you have cause to reprove someone. If the stone stands alone in your nightmare, often it represents the self.

Storm

To dream of an approaching storm indicates emotional turmoil in some aspect of your life. Dark skies and thunder might also be a forewarning that danger is approaching. Alternately, a storm could symbolize rapid changes occurring in your life.

Suffocation

To dream of being suffocated may have to do with the way you're sleeping. Is your breathing being obstructed in some way, by a cold, asthma, or a blanket? If not, it's possible you fear being bossed around or caged in. Other people or circumstances may be suppressing your expression.

Suicide

A dream of killing yourself probably is a symbolic reflection of what's going on in your conscious life. Such a dream might reflect a personal transformation: a divorce, changing careers, or other major life shifts. You are essentially killing your past and becoming a new person.

Sword

A sword can cut to the bone. A frightening dream in which a sword is featured might suggest that aggressive action is required.

T

Teeth

A nightmare about losing teeth might be a literal warning about your dental condition. But if you've had a checkup, then you should consider that the bad dream might be telling you something about yourself.

Teeth are what you use to bite. If you lose your bite, you lose power. Losing teeth might also symbolize a loss of face or spoiled self-image. It could also be a metaphor for "loose" or careless speech. Note the other aspects of the dream. For example, to examine your teeth suggests that you exercise caution in a matter at hand. To clean your teeth indicates that some struggle is necessary to keep your standing. Admiring your teeth for their whiteness suggests that wishes for a pleasant occupation and happiness will be fulfilled. To dream that you pull your own teeth and are feeling around the cavity with your tongue signifies your trepidation over a situation you are about to enter. Dreaming of imperfect teeth connotes bad feelings about your appearance and well-being.

If those meanings don't work for you, however, ask yourself what teeth mean to you. Do they represent power? A nice appearance? Aggressiveness? What is it, exactly, that makes you feel "toothless"?

Thief

If you dream of someone stealing something, the implication is that something is being taken from you. It does not necessarily have to be a theft of actual goods. It could be something more abstract, such as a boss or colleague who is stealing your energy or ideas. If you're the thief, the message could be a warning that you are taking what you don't deserve and should change your ways.

Thirst

A bad dream in which you are thirsty suggests that you are in need of nourishment, either physical, mental, or emotional. To see others relieving their thirst suggests that this nourishment might come from others.

Thorn

A thorn can represent an annoyance of some sort—in other words, "a thorn in your side."

Tiger

Aggressive and fierce in the wild, these animals, when they appear in a bad dream, might symbolize that you are under persecution or will be tormented.

Tornado

A swift and terrible agent of destruction in nature, a tornado in a nightmare suggests that your desire for a quick resolution in a matter at hand could lead to disappointment.

Torrent

A nightmare about a seething torrent of water suggests profound unrest in the emotional state of the dreamer or a person in the dream.

Tower

In a nightmare, a tower could symbolize vigilance, as a watchtower, or punishment or isolation, as a guard tower. Dreaming of being in an "ivory tower" indicates that you or the subject of your dream may be out of touch with the everyday world.

Travel

You may have experienced nightmares where traveling was usually the theme. If it was a repetitive dream, especially from a different time period, it may be a past-life experience that ended traumatically. If that is the case, you can use your favored techniques to resolve the nightmare. As you uncover more about past-life traveling dreams, you are also beginning to establish, through conscious awareness, goals for future ones.

Just as any traveler uses past experiences to help him prepare for his next journey, your previous travel dream experiences can help you create travel plans for your next lucid travel dream. By reviewing past experiences, you may become aware of pitfalls to avoid in the future. If you have experienced lucid travel dreams before, you may not have known that you could control them.

Trial

A nightmare about being on trial suggests that you are being judged, or you are afraid of being judged. Alternately, a trial in a dream could indicate that you are judging others too harshly.

Tunnel

From a Freudian perspective, a dream of a tunnel suggests a vagina, and a train entering the tunnel represents sexual intercourse. Usually, however, a tunnel shows you moving from one part of life to another, but you can't see the outcome yet. A tunnel may also be a link between two conditions. When you exit the tunnel, you will enter a new state of mind.

U

UFO

The UFO reminds you of your place as a citizen of a very large universe. Dreaming of a UFO might also indicate something unusual or foreign affecting your life.

Ugly

If you or someone in your nightmare is ugly, you feel unattractive. Or, you don't like your own or someone else's behavior. This bad dream could also point to an unhealthy trait that you or another possess. You may also fear rejection based on superficial criteria.

Ulcer

If you dream you have an ulcer, something is eating at you. What in your waking life is bothering you? If the ulcer is bleeding in the nightmare, the situation is sapping your life force. Change the situation, or your reaction to it, if at all possible.

Underground

To dream of being in an underground habitation often symbolizes contact with your subconscious. Other images in the dream will provide more meaning as to the nature of the contact. Is there something you've been hiding that should be brought to the surface? Ask yourself how you feel about the situation. Are you being held prisoner or hiding? Dreaming of an underground railway could indicate passage to another state of being, a personal transformation. Examine the events of your life to see how such an interpretation would fit.

Unemployment/Unemployed

If you have a nightmare about being unemployed, this could represent literal events transpiring in your waking life at the time. More likely you are releasing fears that you won't have meaningful work or that the work you do won't support you. If you dream you are on an unemployment line, you feel you have to rely on others for your survival.

Urination

A nightmare in which you urinate may simply indicate that you need to wake up and go to the bathroom. Symbolically, the dream may represent a desire to eliminate impurities from your life.

V

Vagrant

Are you afraid of losing your home, stability, or livelihood?
Perhaps you want to break away from social regimentation.

Vampire

To dream of a vampire might indicate that someone is
draining energy from you or taking advantage of you. The
message is to guard against people who take too much of
your time or energy. To dream of battling or staking a
vampire suggests a positive outcome versus someone with
harmful intentions.

Veil

A nightmare in which someone or something is veiled suggests that you're hiding something or something is being
hidden from you.

Veins

Veins are like tributaries that carry blood to the extremities.
If you dream your veins are blocked, you feel your vitality or
life force is blocked in a certain area—work, creativity, relationships, and so on. If your veins are discolored in the bad
dream, you may not feel fully energized and alive; you aren't
sending energy throughout all parts of your life.

Ventriloquist

If you dream of a ventriloquist, beware of deception and fraud. Dreaming of a ventriloquist can also mean that a love affair might turn out badly for you.

Verdict

If you dream of a verdict, you feel judged and believe what happens in your life is up to someone other than you. If you deliver a verdict, you have strong ideas about what other people should do, and want to control someone else's behavior. You may also feel you are being treated unfairly in a situation. Or, you might believe you have done something wrong for which you need to be judged or punished.

Victim

A dream in which you are some sort of victim might indicate that you're feeling helpless regarding a situation. If someone rescues you, the dream suggests that help is available.

Voices

If you hear angry voices in your nightmares, think about where you are frustrated or angry with yourself or others.

If the voices are sad, you need to process and release sadness or grief.

Volcano

The eruption of a volcano or a smoking volcano might suggest your strong emotions are rising to the surface and need to be expressed before you explode.

Vomit

To vomit in a nightmare might be a dramatic exhibition of a need to rid something or someone from your life. To dream of vomiting a chicken suggests an illness in a relative will be a cause of disappointment. To see others vomiting symbolizes that someone's false pretenses will soon be made apparent.

Vulture

A dream that includes a vulture indicates that a predator is nearby.

W

Waiting

Waiting in a dream is a sign that you are not in control of whatever it is you want to happen. Perhaps you are waiting for someone else or waiting for a situation to change. Waiting usually brings with it feelings of impatience and frustration, so think about where you are waiting in life and what you can do to move things forward.

Walls

Walls, like fences, can protect or block. Where are the walls in your nightmare and why are they there? If you need better emotional boundaries, you may dream of putting up a wall. You may also dream you are putting up a wall to keep someone from you, or that someone you know is putting up walls in your relationship. Fears of intimacy could cause you to wall yourself off from your own happiness. This dream might also suggest you need better boundaries in your relationships.

War

A dream of war could relate to reliving your past in the military. Whether you've served in the military or not, a dream of war might symbolize internal turmoil or a need to make peace with yourself, or others. By examining other elements in the dream, you might be able to determine the message behind the aggressive behavior. Because death is often imminent in war-torn situations, a dream that includes war images might also have to do with going through tough changes or transitions. (See also *Death*.)

Water

Consider your emotional state when you have water symbols in your nightmares. If you dream you are drowning, you feel overwhelmed emotionally at this time in your life. If you dream you are trapped in ice or snow, your emotions have hardened and you are having difficulty identifying and releasing them. If the water in your dream is warm, pleasant, and cleansing, you are feeling emotionally balanced at this time in your life.

To dream of muddy water means your feelings about a certain person or situation are not clear. If the water is clear, you know what your heart desires. Rough water may connote problems communicating or getting along with a loved one.

Weapon

Weapons may stand for the male genitals. Notice who is holding the weapon and how it is being used. Context is very important for determining the meaning behind weapons in dreams.

Weeds

Dreaming of weeds suggests that something needs to be weeded out from your life. An overgrown garden might signify that something is being neglected in your life. If you have a bad dream that features tangled weeds, it indicates a need for cleansing or purification.

Well

A nightmare about falling into a well symbolizes a loss of control regarding a matter at hand. A dry well indicates you feel a part of your life is empty and needs to be nourished. To draw water from a well denotes the fulfillment of emotional desires.

Whip

Being whipped in a dream refers to two things: You feel you deserve punishment for some transgression, or you feel someone is taking advantage of you undeservedly. If you dream of whipping someone, beware of your own manipulative or aggressive tendencies.

Whirlpool

Water represents the emotions or the unconscious, so to dream of a whirlpool might indicate that your emotions are in a state of flux and can ensnarl you unless caution is exercised.

Whirlwind

A dream of a whirlwind suggests that you are confronting a change in a matter at hand that threatens to overwhelm you. Pay attention to the other aspects of the dream. Are you facing this danger alone or with somebody else? Are you in your house or another location?

Wind

If you dream you are walking against a brisk wind, it indicates you are courageous, resist temptations, and pursue your hopes with a plucky determination. You will be successful. If, however, in your dream the wind blows you along against your wishes, it signifies you might have disappointments in love and in business.

Winter

Winter is often synonymous with the yearly death of nature, after its three seasons of regeneration, growth, and harvest. Winter is also a time for hibernation or slowing down. If you dream of winter, consider if you have recently gone through any sort of metaphoric death. Have you recently ended a relationship or put a bad situation or habit behind you?

Witch

The Halloween image of a witch might be symbolic of a scary or evil scenario. Your brain may be telling you that you have fears you have not admitted to yourself.

Wolf

In Native American lore, the wolf is good medicine, a symbol of the pathfinder, a teacher with great wisdom and knowledge. Dreaming of a wolf can be auspicious. But in a nightmare, the wolf can be a symbol of a lone male aggressively pursuing a young female as in the Little Red Riding Hood fable.

Y

Yell/Yelling

If you find yourself yelling at someone in your nightmare, it represents unexpressed anger or frustration either at yourself, another person, or a situation in your life that you feel unable to change. If you are being yelled at in your dream, you feel others are judging you. If you hear someone yelling from a distance in your dream, you may unconsciously be asking for help.

Yellow

This color can be linked to cowardly behavior.

Yoke

If you dream of a yoke or see yourself yoked in a nightmare, it means that you feel compelled to do things for and/or with others. You may feel you can't rely on your own power alone or accomplish your goals by yourself. To whom do you feel bound? Where are you following the directions of others in your waking life? If you are experiencing a transition in your life, this transition may have been thrust upon you and is not one you like (for example, a divorce you didn't initiate).

YouTube

Having a nightmare about being publicly humiliated on YouTube means what is going on in your life is for public display. If you feel worried in the dream, you feel parts of your life that you would prefer to remain hidden are being revealed.

Z

Zero

A symbol of many interpretations, zero can mean emptiness, a lack of something in your life. It also forms a circle and can stand for wholeness and completion, or even the mysteries of the unknown. In Freudian terms, the shape is reminiscent of a vagina and suggests a desire for sexual relations.

Zoo

A scary dream that takes place in a zoo might relate to a feeling of being in a cage. It could also symbolize chaos: "This place is like a zoo."

PART 3
Nightmare Journal

_____

_____

_____

_____

_____

_____

_____

_____

_____

_____

_____

_____

_____

_____

_____

_____

_____

_____

_____

_____

_____

_____

_____

_____

_____

_____

_____

_____

PART 3: NIGHTMARE JOURNAL

THE NIGHTMARE DICTIONARY

272

_____
_____
_____
_____
_____
_____
_____
_____
_____
_____
_____
_____
_____
_____
_____
_____
_____
_____
_____
_____
_____
_____
_____
_____
_____
_____
_____
_____
_____

PART 3: NIGHTMARE JOURNAL

_____

_____

_____

_____

_____

_____

_____

_____

_____

_____

_____

_____

_____

_____

_____

_____

_____

_____

_____

_____

_____

_____

_____

_____

_____

_____

_____

_____

_____

_____

_____

APPENDIX A
GLOSSARY OF TERMS

Akashic records
An imaginary book believed to hold every deed, word, feeling, thought, and intent of every soul in the universe

Conscious mind
The surface of the mind; the communication center where you process thoughts and ideas

DILD
Dream-induced lucid dream

Dream
Sensory images experienced while a person is asleep

Future pacing
A term in hypnosis used to deepen your altered state of consciousness by a suggestion anticipating a positive response

Guided imagery
The process of inducing a trance or altered state of consciousness

Hypnagogic state
Transition between wakefulness and sleep, also spelled hypnogogic

Hypnosis
An altered state of consciousness in which the unconscious mind accepts suggestions

Lucid
Being consciously aware of one's thoughts

Lucid dream
Being aware while you are in a dream

Mantra
A word or a phrase repeated over and over to help raise the spiritual vibrational level of the participant

Medium
A person through whom the deceased can communicate with the living

MILD
Mnemonic-induced lucid dreams

Mind's eye
Images created in the mind through the five senses of seeing, hearing, feeling, tasting, and smelling

Nightmare
A dream that causes the dreamer to experience fear

Other side
The world of spirits and the dead that exists on another
plane of reality than the normal world

Power of suggestion
A suggestion that others accept as real without actual proof

Psychic
The ability to obtain information from sources that have
no scientifically proven basis, such as intuition or the
supernatural

Reality
Something that can be proven to exist

REM
Rapid eye movement; it is most intense in the latter stage of a dream

Self–hypnosis
The process of inducing a trance state in yourself

Unconscious mind
The storage area of the mind that contains all your past experiences; also referred to as the subconscious

Underworld
In shamanism, a place below the earth's surface where power animals are believed to exist and where humans came from and return to after death

APPENDIX B

BOOKS FOR FURTHER READING

Castaneda, C., *The Art of Dreaming*. New York, HarperCollins, 1993.

Delaney, G., *Breakthrough Dreaming: How to Tap the Power of Your 24-Hour Mind*. New York, Bantam, 1991.

Faraday, A., *Dream Power*. New York, Afar Publishers, 1972.

Faraday, A., *The Dream Game*. New York, Harper & Row, 1974.

Garfield, P., *Creative Dreaming*. New York, Ballantine, 1974.

Godwin, M., *The Lucid Dreamer*. New York, Simon & Schuster, 1994.

Harner, M., *The Way of the Shaman*. New York, Harper & Row, 1980.

Jung, C., Memories, *Dreams, Reflections*. New York, Vintage, 1961.

Jung, C., *Man and His Symbols*. New York, Dell, 1964.

LaBerge, S., *Lucid Dreaming*. New York, Ballantine, 1986.

LaBerge, S. and Rheingold, H., *Exploring the World of Lucid Dreaming*. New York, Random House, 1990.

Lewis, J., *The Dream Encyclopedia*. Detroit, Visible Ink Books, 1995.

Maxmen, J., *A Good Night's Sleep*. New York, Warner, 1981.

McGuire, W. and Hull, R. (Eds.), C.G. *Jung Speaking*. Princeton, NJ, Princeton University Press, 1977.

Michaels, S., *The Bedside Guide to Dreams*. New York, Fawcett Crest, 1995.

Morris, J., *The Dream Workbook*. New York, Fawcett Crest, 1985.

Perkins, J., *PsychoNavigation*. Rochester, VT, Destiny Books, 1990.

Perkins, J., *The World as You Dream It: Shamanic Teachings from the Amazon and Andes*. Rochester, VT, Destiny Books, 1994.

Roberts, J., *Seth Speaks*. New York, Prentice-Hall, 1972.

Roberts, J., *The Nature of Personal Reality: A Seth Book*. New York, Prentice-Hall, 1974.

Roberts, J., *Seth: Dreams and Projection of Consciousness*. New York, Prentice-Hall, 1987.

Sanford, J., *Dreams and Healing: A Succinct and Lively Interpretation of Dreams*. New York, Paulist Press, 1978.

Ullman, M. and Krippner, S. and Vaughan, A., *Dream Telepathy*. Toronto, Macmillan, 1973.

Ullman, M., and Zimmerman, N., *Working with Dreams*. New York, Dell, 1979.

Villoldo, A., *Dance of the Four Winds*. New York, Harper & Row, 1990.

Villoldo, A., *Island of the Sun: Mastering the Inca Medicine Wheel.* San Francisco, HarperSanFrancisco, 1992.

Williams, S., *Jungian-Senoi Dreamwork Manual.* Berkeley, Journal Press, 1980.

INDEX

INDEX